PRESENCE

THE TRUTH OF YOGA

by Ruth White

PRESENCE

THE TRUTH OF YOGA

by Ruth White

PRESENCE · THE TRUTH OF YOGA

By Ruth White

Edited by Fiona Stuart

Copyright © Ruth White 2017

Published by Darien-Jones Publishing.

Designed, illustrated and produced by Nick Darien-Jones of Nicholas J Jones Graphics.

Book design ©2017 Nicholas J Jones Graphics.

A CIP catalogue record for this book is available from the British Library.

ISBN 978-1-902487-10-6

The author and publisher have made all reasonable efforts to contact copyright holders for permission, and apologise for any omissions or errors in the text matter, quotations and extracts in this book. Corrections may be made to further printings.

Printed using papers made from trees that have been legally sourced from well-managed and credibly certified forests.

Jacket photograph of Ruth White by Richard Beal.

Darien-Jones Publishing
PUBLISHERS OF MAPS & BOOKS

Telephone: (01452) 812550 Fax: (01452) 812690
E-mail: sales@darien-jones.co.uk
www.darien-jones.co.uk

**Yoga With
Ruth White**

Email: info@yogawithruthwhite.com
www.yogawithruthwhite.com

CONTENTS

FOREWORD

I have been blessed in knowing Ruth White for many years. I first met her while teaching a meditation class in early 1999. I was immediately drawn to her unique combination of profound experience and knowledge, coupled with a deep humility and desire to experience the true nature of the Self.

On the Monday after that short weekend, Ruth immediately invited me to a Greek island to experience her yoga retreat and to share meditation with her students who were interested. 'When do we leave?' I asked. 'Wednesday,' she replied matter-of-factly. This was my first experience of her attentiveness to the present moment – no other plans could possibly matter. And that was true.

While I had done yoga before, that retreat showed me a whole new world of what yoga really was. Ruth's ability to teach a class of forty students and give individual attention to each was something I had not experienced, and still have not experienced with anyone else to this day. Her knowledge of the body and how the postures affect change is, in my experience, unsurpassed. How she can look at a physical body and see the beliefs and judgements which create the stiffness and physical problems is truly amazing.

What stands out above all else with Ruth is the understanding that yoga has so little to do with physical movements. She knows to the core of her being that true yoga is union with the absolute Self. She has spent most of her life in pursuit of that experience.

Over the years that have passed since we first met, I have been lucky to spend a great deal of time with Ruth. Her commitment to discovering the true nature of reality is unwavering. Intellectual understanding is not enough; she lives to *experience* truth. That is the rarest of human perspectives.

This book weaves together Ruth's life-long experience of yoga practice as a way to transcend limiting beliefs and positions, her passion for the path of consciousness that is true yoga and her dedication to her own experience of the endless silent presence that exists forever beyond the movements of the linear mind. All of this she shares with her light and innocent clarity and humour.

Whether you are a lifelong yogi, a teacher or student of yoga, or if you have never even considered bending down to touch your toes, there is wisdom in this book for everyone.

Narain Ishaya

Author of *Chit Happens: A Guide to Discovering Divinity*

THANKS

How fortunate I am to have a husband and three wonderful children who have practised and supported me throughout this yoga journey and continue to do so.

Karuna runs a yoga centre in Perth, Australia, Christina a centre in Stratford-upon-Avon and Roland runs Healthtext. John and I teach here in the Cotswolds and around the world.

Grateful thanks to my friend, Fiona Stuart, for her patience and understanding in translating a dyslexic's notes. This book would not have been written without her.

Ruth White

Website: www.yogawithruthwhite.com

email: info@yogawithruthwhite.com

The White family – From the left, top John and Roland,
bottom Ruth, Christina and Karuna.

Ruth White

INTRODUCTION

T his book is about how we can change the way we think. It is a guide to coming back to our natural state, where we are free from worldly worries and imagined problems. When the mind quietens down, our hearts automatically open and we are able to experience the bliss of the present moment. It is then that we can wake up to the truth – that we are just as we should be, at home and at peace with the world.

I have been teaching the practice of yoga for over fifty years and all the references and practical examples given here are drawn from personal experience. As a teenager I was inspired by my teacher, B.K.S. Iyengar[1], an enlightened man. Through him I learned that each of the eight limbs of yoga[2] echoes its real meaning, which is to quieten the fluctuations of the mind.

What is enlightenment? It is but a recognition that the spiritual light is shining in us now. It is not something we have to search for, come to and eventually attain after years of study and practice. It is our birthright. Presence – we might also use the word God or Higher Self – shines in every living creature. It is our home, our source. It is never diminished or made greater. It is eternal.

---

1 B.K.S. Iyengar (14 December 1918 – 20 August 2014), one of the foremost yoga teachers in the world. See Appendix.
2 See Appendix for a detailed description of Patanjali's Eight-fold Path of Yoga.

The only reason we suffer in life is because of attachment and for many people, especially yogis, it might be their attachment to the body. Once, when we were in the middle of standing postures in a yoga class, I noticed that one of the participants, a seventy-year old woman, had started to cry. I went over to her and asked if she needed help. 'I'm too old,' she said. 'I can't do what I used to do.' She was attached to her transient body, attached to the memory, to the past. She could not see how she was shining with *Sat, Chit, Ananda*[3] – Truth, Consciousness and Bliss. We are all shining with that.

Here's a friendly warning! Our attitudes *can* change and as they do we find we are beginning to feel more loving, tolerant, peaceful and free, or as one student said, 'It's funny, but there are no aggravating people any more'. Another student came into class looking quite beautiful, her face unlined. Her homework had been to look at the pointlessness of worrying and to stop the habit. Noticeably, it had worked.

The transient world has its lifetime; it is born and dies. It comes and goes, but the Light never goes, is not born and does not die. Whether we realise it or not it is permanent, eternal.

---

3 *Sat, Chit, Ananda:* the three Sanskrit words that describe pure, undifferentiated non-duality.

INTENTION AND THE PRACTICE OF YOGA

Yoga classes tend to arise when there is an imbalance in society. It often happens in large cities where life can appear to speed up and where peace of mind becomes clouded over by desires and forward thinking. Conversely, it is often in more rural areas that the beauty of nature can bring our attention back to the present moment and so life slows down. By being still and attentive in this way we are taken out of the hustle and bustle of the mind and come to rest in the unchanging, eternal 'now'.

A person with good intention may be inspired to meet the needs of others and start a yoga school; in this way an organisation grows up, working for the community and not for personal gain. However, the yin and yang[4] of it is that if, somewhere along the line, someone in the school starts to work for personal aggrandisement then the whole community changes.

It's a bit like my bees. If I get a bad-tempered queen the whole hive takes on her characteristics and I have to watch out, but if I then change the queen for a good-natured one the whole feeling and the sound of the hive changes within an hour, becoming peaceful and harmonious. The hum drops to a melodious pitch and the worker

4 Taoist symbols. Yin (shady side) and Yang (sunny side) illustrate the concept of duality forming a whole – of how opposite forces are connected and complementary, giving rise to each other as they interrelate.

bees calm down and are happy. Similarly, when society becomes unbalanced (we don't just bump off our queen!) we look around for inspiration. If this is important enough for us – I mean if the need and yearning to feel happy, at home, centred and loving is strong enough – we will seek the company of like-minded people and it is then probable that an enlightened person will arise, one who has already realised his or her true nature.

This book is about our journey back to Heaven[5]. Actually, we have never left it so our work is simply to clear away the clouds that obscure the truth. All the bumps and hiccups we experience along the way can be regarded as opportune challenges. Of course, the line our ego[6] would take to such a suggestion would be to react adversely to it, seeking to justify and maintain our habitual behaviour and attitudes.

Alternatively, we could just *observe* what's happening (for example, how we are becoming angry and critical) and watch each situation unfurl without judging our behaviour. It's our choice as to how we treat a particular situation; we could regard it as a learning curve, a lesson, and so feel the freedom of not being attached to the outcome. On the other hand, if we become involved and identified with it then that situation could become our nightmare or prison.

It might be helpful to catch the reflection you see of yourself in others. Ponder the words of the writer and philosopher, William Hazlitt (1778-1830): 'Just as much as we see in others we have in ourselves.'

Chasing wealth and opulence can be a great disadvantage as the 'want it/got it' race goes on. There is no end or satisfaction in climbing towards a summit which is for ever out of reach and further away.

---

5 Heaven: the dwelling place of God; our home; an awareness of perfect Oneness, as defined in *A Course in Miracles*, written and edited by Helen Schucman. (Website: www.acim.org)
6 Ego: our imagined thoughts.

The simple practice of yoga can change values and priorities, so we should take stock of what we really want in life more than anything else and go for it! Why not?

Do you know anyone who is unhappy with his or her situation, job, partner or home? Perhaps it's the same for you. How easily the ego mind can cook up some story, perhaps about your life not being perfect; it encourages you to think that if you worry over things for long enough your life will change magically to the way you imagine it should be and then you will be happy. Well, that's all an exhausting illusion.

Yet there is something we can all do to change our attitude to the world: we can take a step back and look again at the situation that's bugging us. Is it our thoughts and our judgements about it that are making us unhappy? Are all these thoughts *really* true? When we learn to observe what is going on in our minds we develop the ability to let go of these ideas and criticisms and that is when the miracle[7] happens – it's like turning on a switch. We come out of our mental prison and the whole world changes. Mind stuff is never true.

If you are a new yoga student you will primarily need to work with the visible outer body, but as you continue to practise and watch you learn to understand and see with the inner eye how the organs are working and how, if you move your inner body, it can take you further into a posture. In a twist, you turn your chest to the right as far as you can and then when you think you have turned to your limit you move behind the breast bones – your heart, your inner body, even further.

My teacher, B.K.S. Iyengar, would say that true knowledge comes from observation – experiencing the now. When, with complete attention, we are practising *asanas* (postures), then all the other seven

7 *A Course in Miracles* defines the word 'miracle' as the shift in perception from fear to love.

limbs of Patanjali's Eight-fold Path of Yoga are present; so too are our physical, mental and spiritual bodies. Yet we are really working to change our attitude, for once the mind is convinced we can perform any *asana* then we will be able to do so. When we give our complete attention in this way the mind begins to quieten down and we are able to listen and understand what our bodies are showing us. Then we may realise that although our 'bespoke' body is indeed a wonderful tool to work with, yet it can do nothing without the mind's permission. The only reason we can't perform a posture is because we think we can't. When gathering us together, Iyengar would laugh and say, 'Come on, my mental class'. At first I felt a little discouraged by his comment, but I soon began to understand what he actually meant. He was right.

As we work in the *asanas*, perhaps stretching a little further than we normally do or holding for longer, we can actually stretch out of limiting ideas (in truth, there are no limitations); as we wake up the inactive, *tamasic*[8] parts of the body and calm down the more *rajasic*, overworked areas we bring our physical body into balance. In this balanced state of mind, with fewer limitations, our horizons widen.

---

8 In Vedanta philosophy the *gunas* (the three qualities of Nature that underlie matter, life and mind) consist of *tamas* (passive force), *rajas* (active force) and *sattva* (neutralising force). Further references to the *gunas* occur in the book.

LISTEN TO YOUR HEART

Here's an interesting fact: When the mind falls quiet the heart opens automatically. This especially happens to me after practising *pranayama* (control of the breath), when I feel very loving and know that I am loved.

It is a joy to teach a yoga class from the heart, yet mental limitations begin to impose themselves as soon as I turn to thinking. A while ago, Sharon, one of my student teachers, was taking a holiday class in which many of those present were faced with great challenges. Usually she teaches spontaneously from the heart, but as she stood in front of the class, ready to teach *asana* practice, she was overcome by fear. She had started to doubt her ability to look after the participants' diverse needs. She stood there speechless; the words just didn't come. Fortunately, though after what to her felt like an eternity, she realised what was happening – that she had disappeared into her thoughts. In that instant of realisation she went back to teach from her heart, the knowledge flowed and the class progressed beautifully. Everyone in the group was loved and cared for.

It is the same with us when we are practising yoga or meditation. If we become aware of anxieties creeping in we need to bring our attention back to the posture or mantra or whatever we are engaged in and if we are able to be *whole*-hearted about this then fears and ideas will simply dissolve away.

I have noticed that when yoga students are standing in front of a class, about to teach and take their final assessment, it is fear that often masks their skills. Wanting to put them at their ease and allow their talents to shine I discovered that the *only* way to dissolve fear is to allow the love to flow between teacher and students; in other words, to go back to the stillness which is always there. Our anxious imaginings of what could go wrong can temporarily obscure this stillness. How strange it is to want to create our own fearful world rather than live in peace. As with Sharon's example, as soon as we come out of the heart and go up to the head the awareness of the present moment disappears. True teaching must come through our quiet heart centre which manifests pure love. Then knowledge will flow and the words just come.

We should allow ourselves to rest in the silence. We should trust it. It's OK to have nothing, just space; it can actually feel comfortable to be devoid of thought. Out of it will come the naked truth, free from the cloak of the ego mind.

I have come to the conclusion that we can't teach people *how* to teach but rather we can show them how to come out of the busy head into their hearts. It has been said that the longest journey we will make, eighteen inches, is from our head to our heart, but it could happen instantaneously. Every limb of yoga is advocating that we make that journey. With practice it will not take too long.

Most students are able to recognise where their teacher is coming from. If the teacher appears to be serious, with no empathy, then the instruction will often fall short, whereas a teacher, teaching from the heart, who is loving, bright and cheerful, connects with her or his students and the truth is conveyed.

Please don't waste time thinking about what others think of you. Just express love and the knowledge will pass between you. We lose so much energy by worrying about the future, imagining our shortcomings and thinking we are not able to cope in a situation. Give your full attention to the situation in front of you rather than allowing yourself to suffer from something that may never happen. Remember that love dissolves fear and enables true communication and freedom. Be generous. Love is not love until you give it away.

When I stand in front of a class it is so noticeable that most of the students' so-called physical limitations are actually mental ones. We think we cannot go further, or we criticise ourselves or the teacher, and then as we stray from the present, out of the heart into the head, fear grips the body and holds us back. Remember the Old Testament story of Lot's wife, turned to a pillar of salt because she ignored the angels' warning and looked back to her old life in Sodom? Don't do it!

It is simple really. Stay in the moment. I say simple, but of course it is not always easy as the nature of the mind, with its thoughts and desires, is like quicksilver. Wholehearted practice of the eight limbs of yoga will have the effect of stilling the mind. It is not an *action* of getting rid of or pushing out thoughts: rather it is by paying complete attention to where you are now and not entertaining those thoughts. In a class, the last posture, *shavasana* or corpse posture, is practised lying down. As the body and eyes become still so the mind quietens. If there is a fidget in the body, then there is a fidget in the mind. Similarly, any thought passing through the mind will be reflected by some movement in the body. It may be so small we don't even notice it, but it will be there. In the first *asana (tadasana)*, the mountain posture, we stand with the weight equally divided between the feet, allowing movements to die down and our breathing to deepen. It is really such a relief for us to give full awareness to the balance of the body. It is by applying our attention in this way, using it like a mantra, that the mind quietens down and our hearts open.

'Infinite patience brings immediate results.'
A Course in Miracles

PRANAYAMA

The fourth limb of Patanjali's Eight-fold Path of Yoga is *pranayama*, the control of the breath. This is an essential practice which opens the heart, essential because without deep breathing *asana* practice would be more of a gymnastic exercise. Every cell in the body needs oxygen, yet breath is more than that – it is *prana*, the life force or breath of life. Buddha advised that before meditation we should first cleanse the body. Different *pranayamas* have different functions and all are cleansing. Some *pranayamas* heat the body and lift energy levels, some have a calming and cooling effect, some eliminate mucus and clear the chest, some stimulate and assist circulation while others balance the right and left hemispheres[9] of the brain. Some soothe the nervous system and all are helpful for anaemia as the levels of oxygen in the blood increase.

The practice of *pranayama* is to establish full regular breathing which can, in turn, control the emotions. Therefore a change in the breathing can indicate a change in the emotional state. Take, as an example, a mother who listens to her child's breathing to discover whether the infant is sleeping and/or in good health; with the same quality of attention a yoga teacher will pause before physically

9 The two hemispheres of the brain are joined by the corpus callosum. Generally, the left brain processes language, i.e. what we hear and speak, in recalling facts and is also involved in logic and mathematical calculations. The right hemisphere generally deals with spatial awareness, interpreting visual images and has the function of processing music. As regards language, it interprets context and tone of voice.

correcting a student, taking the individual further into the posture on his or her exhalation; similarly you may notice a change in your own breathing if you are excited, nervous, sad, happy or hurt.

To practise we usually adopt a sitting position where the back is straight and we are comfortable and in balance, warm and free from bodily distractions. The simple practice of conscious deep breathing will have a quietening and stabilising effect. Our *asana* practice is to prepare us for our meditations and *pranayamas*. These meditative practices have the effect of lifting the spirits and opening the heart, allowing our true nature to shine through. It sounds extraordinary but it has the effect of allowing us to see clearly. This is what happens when the mind falls quiet and we begin to listen and look from our hearts.

Listen to your breathing. It will tell you about your emotional state. *Practise* the art of breathing and you can change your emotional state.

ATTENTION AND PRACTICE

'To the mind that is still, the whole universe surrenders.'
Lao Tzu[10]

ONE-POINTED ATTENTION

If we choose to practise *asanas* we will become proficient; likewise, if we choose to focus our attention on worrying we will become excellent worriers. The power of our attention is enormous, so perhaps we need to be careful not to give too much consideration to misfortune.

Iyengar understood the power of positive attention. One day a ten-year old boy came into his yoga class. He had crushed his pelvic girdle and hip in a fall and the medical professionals said he would never walk again. Iyengar took the child's arms and held them round his neck, letting him rest on his back with his feet just touching and dragging along the floor. After a while it was noticeable that as Iyengar moved, so too did the boy's legs start to display movement. He carried the child around in this position while continuing to teach his class of sixty students and it was half an hour before the boy finally lay down to rest. Some of the teachers went over to console the child, expressing their concern that he must be very tired. Was he hurting, they asked? Iyengar, hearing all this, shouted across the room, urging

10 Lao Tzu (died 531 BC) was a Chinese philosopher and writer, the reputed author of the *Tao Te Ching*.

his students to stop: 'He'll never walk if you sympathise and give attention to his so-called failings.'

Because they live in the present moment, small children don't understand adult negativity or deferment. When I gave my son a BMX bicycle for his fifth birthday I told him I would take him to the children's racetrack 'soon'. First thing next morning, before it was even light, I was woken up by a little figure. Wearing his crash helmet, elbow and knee pads and a few clothes, he was leaning over me, asking, 'Shall we go now?' Abstract words like 'later' or 'tomorrow' had no meaning for him.

In my own childhood I noticed how most adults weren't really 'there' when they were talking, choosing rather to be involved with their thoughts. I assumed this was the way all adults behaved and that it would happen to me when I became a grown-up.

GROUP POWER

When like-minded people are working together with one common aim, for example in a yoga practice, it is as if their energies are not just added together – they are multiplied. The participants are lifted by the power of attention, the energy levels and the support they give each other. In *asana* practice you work for each other, so strengthening the ability to hold the posture for longer or take it a little further. By giving complete attention we move into a state of meditation where the ego mind falls quiet. We come into the present – our centre – where our strength lies. Sometimes when this happens I feel I could hold the posture for ever.

What happens when we face challenges in our group practice? If we come across a challenge in the way of a posture or a personality, we can use this to our advantage. It can change our attitude. There is a wonderful story that illustrates the opportunity to change in this way. It happened at Gurdjieff's[11] Institute for the Harmonious Development of Man at Le Prieuré, Fontainebleau. The difficult and challenging behaviour of one of his students, an elderly Russian called Rachmilevitch, was annoying many of the other students. After months of putting up with him, they went to Gurdjieff and complained bitterly, requesting that Rachmilevitch be told to leave Le Prieuré. Gurdjieff responded by advising them that actually Rachmilevitch happened to be the most important group member because his presence was giving everyone the opportunity to observe their own responses; by doing this they would be able to change their attitudes and learn the real meaning of patience, loving kindness and compassion.

For us it is the supposed problems – aches, pains, worries, conflicts – that give us the opportunity to change our attitude and it is when we do change that a little miracle happens. You may notice this occurring when you are practising yoga, particularly in postures that challenge you.

THE IMPORTANCE OF PRACTICE

We are whole, perfect and innocent, just as God made us. When we accept this truth there will be no criticisms, judgements, feelings of guilt or lack of love. It will uncover the fact that we are always in Heaven and have never left it. Practising the eight limbs of yoga brings us to the realisation that underneath all the thinking we are in unity and bliss, *ananda*, and that the feelings of fear, guilt and separation (from our true Being) are all imagined. Our practice is to bring us out of this false world of imagination to our right mind of Oneness and union.

---

11 Georges Ivanovich Gurdjieff (1866-1949) was an influential Russian mystic and spiritual teacher.

Practice is essential to train the mind and what better practice could there be than Patanjali's Eight-fold Path of Yoga. The body is always here and now, reminding us of our Higher Self and union with God. If this union is what we want more than anything else then we will give it first priority and set aside a time and place where we can practise daily and strengthen our resolve. Fears will melt away as practice strengthens our understanding of union and when the attention is completely on the body then we really are in the present moment.

First-hand experience is the only true way to happiness and ultimately enlightenment. I can copy my yoga teacher's instructions, his words and his corrections, but I need to practise and experience them myself to make them my own. Then when I teach others it will be from true understanding.

ADVERSITY

'Sweet are the uses of adversity.'
As You Like It, Act 2, Sc.1

OBSTACLES

While, as children, we might have enjoyed taking part in obstacle races, we tend to spend our adult lives trying to avoid supposed hindrances that may come our way. Yet, instead of avoidance, why not try thinking of 'obstacles' as gifts or lessons? They can offer opportunities to rediscover who we really are. Of course, 'who we really are' isn't easy to describe in words, so let's work on what we are not. A quote from His Holiness Shantananda Saraswati[12] is helpful:

'If you begin to be what you are, you will realise everything, but to begin to be what you are, you must come out of what you are not. You are not those thoughts which are turning, turning in your mind; you are not those changing feelings; you are not the different decisions you make and the different wills you have; you are not the separate ego. Well then, what are you? You will find when you have come out

12 His Holiness Shantananda Saraswati (1913-1997), one of the great spiritual teachers in India, was Shankaracharya of Jyotir Math from 1953-1980. He introduced Advaita philosophy to the Study Society (www.studysociety.org) and the School of Economic Science (www.schooleconomicscience.org). The author has links with both these organisations. The above quote is taken from an audience (at the Jyotir Math ashram) with Dr Francis Roles, then head of the Study Society. The *Record* (a transcript of the audiences) can be read and studied on the Study Society website and with a full Index at www.ouspenskytoday.org

of what you are not, that the ripple on the water is whispering to you 'I am That', the birds in the trees are singing to you 'I am That', the moon and the stars are shining beacons to you 'I am That'. You are in everything in the world and everything in the world is reflected in you, and at the same time you are That – everything.'

Everything is in place in our world, just where it should be and 'obstacles' are providing us with an opportunity to learn. When we experience what we may call a difficult situation, a discipline or a practice can help us to change our attitude towards it. Remember that our essence, pure love, lies beneath all the reflections the world is mirroring for us. It is always there and we can come to realise it.

So go back and experience again the state of mind you were in during meditation or in relaxation after a yoga practice, the state where you felt light, expansive, loving, clear and confident. Experience the feeling that occurs when the untruths drop away and you are free from burdens. Why would you want to take on the so-called worries of the world? There's nothing actually wrong with it; it's just the way you see things.

Love *is* and brings unlimited freedom, happiness and space. In Sanskrit, *akasha* is the eternal space in which objects, our reflections, are perceived. If we tune in, *akasha* can be perceived under and between our thoughts. Yet in giving our attention to thoughts and objects we are not always aware of this true space. Try gazing around in a childlike way; be aware of the space around you, expanding it further and further. It has no limits.

Although nothing apparently changes in the visible world, a miracle will occur when you change your attitude and become free from the bondage of attachments and fear. It is then that you are in the heavenly world of spirit, a world of love, the love that dissolves all fear. So if you voice your truths and give them away to others it can only magnify and strengthen that heavenly world. Who wouldn't choose such a miracle?

PRACTISE FORGIVENESS[13]

If you think a situation is not going exactly to plan, you may start to feel that you are being treated unfairly; that it is outrageous, hurtful or cruel and then you start to suffer from your take on the situation, your judgements, your story. But that story isn't real – you have made it up; it's only happening in your mind. Drop it and let it go. Can you see that it is our attachment to our ideas of how things should be different that causes our suffering? Take a step back into the world of love and look again. It could be that the person and/or situation is calling out for your love. Be free of judgemental, limiting thoughts and expectations. They are all imagined. It's as Shakespeare reminds us in *Hamlet:* '. . . for there is nothing either good or bad but thinking makes it so.' (Act 2, Sc.2)

Of course, all this takes practice and perhaps you can't forgive or let go straight away, but do keep going. There may be 'stuff', a nagging thought for example, that pops up from the past to disturb your peace, but if peace is what you really want then take a fresh look and let those thoughts go. It's the only way. Remember that our suffering is made up.

We should also allow our family and friends to make their own way and this sometimes includes letting our children make mistakes. In the *Bhagavad Gita* (3:35), Krishna says that it is better to do our own life's work imperfectly than to do somebody else's well. In other words, we can't rush around healing the world; we should heal our own mind first.

---

13 Here forgiveness means letting go or standing back.

Forgiveness is still, quiet, accepting and loving and dropping accusations and judgements can release a great weight from our shoulders. Things and people are as they are and it's only our judgements that make them 'wrong'.

See yourself in others. Simply look for the beauty, the kindness and the love – it's always there – and when this change of mind occurs your whole world will change with it. Free from suffering and isolation, you will feel at one with the situation or the person.

To judge or criticise another is only to criticise yourself. So forgive.

STATE OF MIND

BELIEF

What do you think about? How important is it? Everything follows from what you think. In an *asana* class it is my job to coax and convince a student that he or she *can* move into the posture. When a limiting thought enters the mind, such as 'I can't do it', it's the ego talking and 'I can't' actually means 'I won't'!

Yet when we break through a limiting idea there is a release of energy, followed by a feeling of relief and exhilaration. A student teacher was taking her assessment and was asked to teach the half moon posture *(ardha chandrasana)*. When moving from triangle onto one leg she didn't believe she could lift the back leg and so took a transitional step in rather than lifting the leg straight up; it meant that when she was teaching it her new students would always copy this intermediate, unnecessary step. Yet when given much encouragement and persuasion she found to her great surprise that she could gracefully shift the weight onto the forward leg and then the back leg came up easily.

A well-known Bible story tells of the power of faith and belief. It concerns a woman who had been suffering an illness for twelve long years. One day, seeing Jesus pass by and believing that his power would cure her, she pushed her way through the crowd and reached out to touch the hem of his cloak. He stopped immediately, turned and asked, 'Who touched me?' Kneeling before him, the woman explained about her illness and her belief. 'Daughter,' he told her, 'your faith has healed you. Go in peace.' On hearing Christ's words, the woman knew that she would be made whole and so she was. Healing always takes place in the mind of the believer.

For the last twenty years I have made an annual visit to Aura Soma, a magical centre tucked away in the small Lincolnshire village of Tetford. In fact, Aura Soma *is* the village. Here they manufacture healing potions, growing herbs for their curative properties as well as flower and plant essences and oils. While ingredients include crystal energies, Bach homeopathic remedies and prayers, the use of colour is the main theme. Aura Soma's bottled solutions have two colours, with the top half of the solution suspended in oil and the bottom in spring water. There are 105 different colour combinations and it is by your choice that the treatments can proceed. I asked, 'Does it work?' and was told, 'If you believe it does, it does'. I now realise what a profound statement this is. Whatever we really believe in becomes manifest for us. It is *by* our belief that it works.

When I first met Iyengar I was experiencing chronic back problems. He corrected my postures with great dexterity and told me in a commanding voice to practise a particular *asana* every day. His direction and instruction was so positive and powerful that for the next twelve months I never missed a day's practice; when I saw him again on his annual visit my back was better. I had believed that it would work and it did.

It is always so. When a Master speaks the truth and you hear it and believe it then what he says will come true for you. Take Sri Nisargadatta Maharaj[14], the great non-dualist teacher. When asked how he became enlightened he explained that his Guru told him:

'Trust me. I tell you; you are divine.' So he followed his instruction, to focus the mind completely on 'I am', pure Being. Soon 'it all disappeared – myself, my Guru, the life I lived, the world around me. Only peace remained and unfathomable silence'.

LOVE OR FEAR – IT'S OUR CHOICE

Love, complete and whole, has the power to dissolve all lesser emotions: jealousy, for example, or the feeling of being let down or misunderstood. If we love God unconditionally and if our greatest desire is to be at one with Him, then our problems and worries will fade from existence.

Once, when giving a yoga retreat on the Isle of Man, I posed the question: 'What is your greatest challenge?' One student admitted that hers concerned a room in her house. Not only was it so full of her most precious possessions that she couldn't use it, but she also had to insure all the items and keep the room locked. This was proving to be a weight on her shoulders, a real problem in her mind. It had seemed too big a challenge for her to face, but now she realised that in order to be free of this mental burden and have her spacious room back again all it required was to give away her so-called treasures.

Do we all behave like this – storing up our burdens and being fearful to let go of them in case we starve or become destitute? It reminds me of the description of how to catch a monkey. First, fix a pot of peanuts in the ground. This will tempt a monkey to stick its hand in and grasp a big handful of the nuts, but unwilling to release its bulging grip on them and because the mouth of the pot is now too narrow, the monkey is well and truly caught.

14 Sri Nisargadatta Maharaj (1897-1981) lived humbly in Bombay, starting out in life as a store keeper, selling mainly *beedis,* leaf-rolled cigarettes. A collection of his spiritual teachings, including the quotation on this page, can be discovered in the book, *I Am That,* translated by Maurice Frydman.

IS GIVING THE SAME AS RECEIVING?

Yama, the first limb of Patanjali's Eight-fold Path, embraces the practice of non-hoarding *(aparigraha)*. Letting go, which for some might include giving away possessions, can therefore come as both a release and a relief. We would do well to remember that we have a choice: whether to be attached to the transient, material world and suffer, or to be free of these attachments and live in the present moment.

I knew a talented artist who lived alone. Many of her paintings hung on the walls of her cottage, while others were stored away. Unfortunately, she became very ill and no one could discover a reason for it or find a remedy. After a while she sought the advice of the head of her philosophy school. He talked with her at some length and during their conversation he asked what she did with her paintings. When she replied that she kept them all he asked her to go home and either give them away, sell them, or exhibit them for others to enjoy. She acted on his advice and as she started to give her precious paintings away and share the enjoyment of the recipients so she became lighter, freer, happier and eventually recovered from her illness.

Whatever you give away comes back to you. It is *always* so. It may not be in the same form but it will come back. When you give away it's like giving back to yourself. This is a natural law.

WE CREATE OUR OWN WORLD

On another occasion, when I put the question 'What is your greatest challenge?' to a group of people, it was a while before anyone spoke. Finally, a woman aged about fifty stood up. She was on the brink of tears as she told us that it had been her wedding anniversary two days before. She and her husband had been married for twenty-six years and she had prepared a special supper for them as a celebration.

When he arrived home, however, he announced that he had decided to leave her because he was in love with someone else. As she spoke, she was suffering visibly, looking devastated and hurt. Yet the last thing she wanted from us was sympathy; it would have made her story and suffering even worse.

I asked her whereabouts she was hurting and she touched her heart. She was brave enough to look at her fear and pain – to bring back the emotion, to feel it and keep looking at her hurt. At first nothing happened; the fear was black and heavy. It took a while, but she kept looking right into the heart of the suffering and very gradually this hard black knot in her heart started to change. I kept asking her: 'How is it now?' She said it was getting lighter and less dense. More questioning and encouragement to look into the centre followed; the 'hurt' turned from black to red and eventually to white. Her face was changing, too. She looked younger, lighter and she almost smiled.

After fifteen minutes of questioning her about the nature of her pain, she looked surprised and said, 'It's gone'. I asked her what was there. After searching for words she said, 'Nothing'. I asked her to describe the feeling and she said, 'My heart is so full of love that I feel as if I am in love again'. At that the whole room was lifted with joy and compassion. Nothing in her world had altered, only her attitude; yet this in turn had changed her perception of the world. The truth had dawned and she was free of her unhappiness.

I was delighted to meet her again on a retreat a year later. She looked happy. She didn't recognise me at first and when I reminded her of the evening we had spent looking into her challenge, when the fear and pain and suffering in her heart had changed into a feeling of immense joy and love, she said she hadn't noticed the miracle. Perhaps these experiences are happening all the time but it is only by grace that we notice them. In such moments we realise we have a choice: either to slip back into our pain and fear world or step into Heaven.

When I asked a group attending a yoga teacher training weekend that same question, one of the students, Eleanor de Zoysa, confided that she had an enormous fear her husband was going to die. She had been nursing him so lovingly through a serious illness that I sense he might well have died without her care. That weekend she found the courage to publicly admit her fear and when she looked deep into the heart of it and kept looking, with the presence and support of the other students, her fear gradually began to disappear and underneath it her true nature – love – emerged. This is her letter to me, sent one week later:

'Once I'd shed my fear that afternoon I was liberated from all my fears and anxieties completely and since then life has become beautiful again. The teaching is incredible – I've never felt more alive nor more happy. I still have my old office job which I do three days and I teach three evenings and one afternoon. I feel tired after the day job, but the moment I step onto my mat in the evening and start to speak I feel both peaceful and energised at the same time and the class just flows. It's such an incredible feeling. Maybe I needed to wait for ten years until I was ready to teach! Thank you for all that you have taught me/us. Although now I am teaching I realise I will never stop learning.'

These examples bring us back to the same thing, namely that all our fear and suffering is imagined. Shakespeare expresses it so clearly in *A Midsummer Night's Dream* (Act 5, Sc.1):

'How in the night, imagining some fear,
How easy is a bush suppos'd a bear?'

To get back to our true nature we have to look at the fear, hate, blame, guilt and anger and see that all this is really in our heads, never in the present moment. The event has already gone or has not yet come and in understanding that we realise we can let the suffering go. It is up to us to choose whether to hang on to the pain or to see through it and realise our true nature, which underneath it all is always the same.

Of course, rather than face a fear, our ego mind will find some diversion, telling us that we are too busy and that now is not the right moment; yet now is the *only* moment and by returning to it there is neither past nor future.

What then *is* the present moment? Nothing but love. Call it what you will – the kingdom of Heaven, divine spark, God, Higher Self or right mind. So if you are in the grip of fear and feeling in despair, remember that your Higher Self is always there to help. All you need to do is ask.

'Truth is within ourselves; it takes no rise
From outward things, whate'er you may believe:
There is an inmost centre in us all,
Where truth abides in fullness;'
Robert Browning (from Paracelsus)

HEAVEN ON EARTH

'The kingdom of Heaven is spread on the face of the
earth, but we do not see it.'
Gospel of Thomas, 113

THE PRODIGAL SON

It is most important to realise where our true treasure lies. Christ's words guide us: 'Lay not up for yourselves treasures upon earth, where moth and rust doth corrupt, and where thieves break through and steal; but lay up for yourselves treasure in Heaven . . . for where your treasure is, there will your heart be also.' (Matthew 6: 19-21)

These words are illustrated so well in the story of the Prodigal Son, the young man who left his father's home (we can understand this as 'heavenly' home) to gain in the material world but as a result suffered scarcity and lack. The story allows us to see through the manifest world of duality to the Oneness and the wholeness of our real home in Heaven. It is when the imagined past and future of the ego mind drop away that we experience the freedom of the eternal Oneness. The world of time and space, desire and lack are no more.

In realising our treasure, the answer is to return home. By definition, the Oneness of our heavenly home is bountiful and complete and we lack nothing. We know that we only suffer from our attachments, yet are we not quite besotted and involved with this incredible creation?

We make it real and so we suffer. Making plans, having expectations, possessions and special relationships all belong to the transitory world. Our heavenly home is all we have. Don't be an absent landlord – live here in the present.

This following description of the Prodigal Son story appears in *The Disappearance of the Universe*[15]:

'There was a man who had two sons; and the younger of them said to the father, 'Father, give me the share of property that falls to me'. And he divided his living between them. Not many days later, the younger son gathered all he had and took his journey into a far country, and there he squandered his property in loose living. And when he had spent everything a great famine arose in that country, and he began to be in want. So he went and joined himself to one of the citizens of that country, who sent him into his fields to feed swine. And he would gladly have fed on the pods that the swine ate; and no one gave him anything. But when he came to himself he said, 'How many of my father's hired servants have bread enough and to spare, but I perish here with hunger! I will arise and go to my father, and I will say to him, "Father, I have sinned against heaven and before you; I am no longer worthy to be called your son; treat me as one of your hired servants".' And he arose and came to his father. But while he was yet at a distance, his father saw him and had compassion, and ran and embraced him and kissed him. And the son said to him, 'Father, I have sinned against heaven and before you; I am no longer worthy to be called your son.' But the father said to his servants, 'Bring quickly the best robe, and put it on him; and put a ring on his hand, and shoes on his feet; and bring the fatted calf and kill it, and let us eat and make merry; for this my son was dead, and is alive again; he was lost, and is found.' And they began to make merry.'

15 *The Disappearance of the Universe*, by Gary R. Renard.

It's really up to you where you want to build your treasure and where you choose will have its own outcome. It is in your hands, in your attitude. You can choose to judge the world, which leads to fear and separation, or to be forgiving, which joins you back to the loving, real world. 'As we see that everyone is still as God created them – whole, perfect and complete – we heal and are healed.' (*A Course in Miracles,* Ch. 14:5) In truth there is no choice as what is permanent, whole and complete can have no opposite.

REMEMBERING

In one of his audiences, Shantananda Saraswati provided Dr Roles, head of the Study Society, with an illustration of where our true treasure lies. He said that all our troubles come from not remembering our Higher Self[16]: 'It is as if each of us possessed two houses. One is a tiny little house, nothing in it, bars on the windows, and in that house we live all our lives.' He went on to explain that the other house is magnificent, containing all that we could want, and yet we forget that we own it. 'If only we could remember that we owned also this other house, we would not be content with living in the little house all the time. When we start to meditate we gradually come out of the little house and we sit for a time between the two houses. When we transcend everything that belongs to our personal life and reach the stage of absolute silence, we are sitting between the two houses without yet realising the big spacious house. If we come out of the little house often enough, and sit for long enough, the memory of the big and spacious house will begin to come to us; we will begin to walk there; we will get a glimpse of it; we will be able to go in. Once we realise what a wonderful house it is we will never want to go back

16 Taken from Dr Roles' description (*Record* 1/6/1961) of his first meeting with Shantananda Saraswati.

to the little house. So, memory of this great big house is self-remembering, but it is not the same as realisation. Self-remembering is remembering the existence of this big house; realisation is when you go in and live there.' *(Record)*

When we are living permanently in the silence of our big house we can communicate directly with God. 'As we study the subject of prayer deeply, we discover that nothing we say to God or think about God ever reaches Him. The only thing that reaches God is a stillness and a silence into which God can flow. God is not in the whirlwind; God is not in the noises of this world; God is not in the mumbo jumbo of our thoughts or words: God is in the "still small voice". So, rightly understood, prayer is an attitude that opens us to receptivity to God's grace. Answered prayer comes only when there is an impartation from within to our awareness – not when something goes out *from* us to God, but when something comes *to* us from God.' *(A Course in Miracles)*

In these moments of awareness, when we rise above the mind, the barriers fall away and we are in the presence of our Higher Self – God. There is no separation, communication is complete and we are one with truth itself.

THE BODY HELPS US TO REMEMBER

I was teaching yoga in Kerala Beach, southern India, when one morning I noticed that the two young Ayurvedic practitioners who were attending to our group looked particularly bright and happy. As I talked to them I realised they were in a higher state and when they explained that they had visited an enlightened monk the previous evening I asked if it would be possible to meet him. They readily agreed, suggesting that four more students might like to accompany us on the trip.

The two boys, riding on bikes and wearing face masks to avoid the pollution in Kerala town, led the way for the two-hour journey. We stopped to buy flowers, fruit – small red bananas, so delicious – and joss sticks; also jasmine wreaths that smelt quite heavenly and would be most appropriate for adorning the grand bronze statues in the temple where the monks lived.

I recall it was very hot and dry in the unyielding sun; there was a tap outside where we ceremoniously washed our feet before entering the cool, quiet space of the outer temple. Here orange-robed monks were kneeling and sitting in lotus position, murmuring their mantras and the Vedas.[17]

We waited for a long time, yet it was so peaceful and welcoming there. Eventually an old, white-whiskered monk appeared and beckoned to us; we followed him into an inner courtyard which was surprisingly barren – a mud yard with two ancient and rickety bamboo huts. One housed the Master and the other was a lavatory. Both had openings for windows. We were allowed to ask one question of the Master. I put my head into the hole in his hut and asked, 'How can I remember?'

At first I could see only two bright, wide-open eyes. Then as he stood I picked out a small, skeletal frame. He was so thin; his arms hung away from his body and he only had a little cloth around his waist. He looked over 100 years old, though I couldn't say exactly how old he was. His presence was awe-inspiring and his eyes so piercing – I can see them now; he spoke in a sharp, quite high voice and in a dismissive way shot out the words, 'The body!' And that was all, so I withdrew my head and went to mull it over.

When the others had asked their questions I couldn't resist putting my head back in the hole and, hoping for a little bit more, asked again,

17 A large body of spiritual texts, originating in ancient India.

'Did you say the body?' He gestured with the back of his hand, repeating 'Yes, you know' three times. Hurriedly I withdrew again, realising much later that he had given me a great present, that it's true we are given a body with all its foibles to look after and it has many ways of waking us up and reminding us to choose Heaven.

I stopped to speak to one of the monks on the way out and he divulged that every morning they had *satsang*[18] in this courtyard with their Master and that, practising together, they all entered *samadhi*[19]. I believe it. On the way home I didn't notice the pollution and my smarting eyes.

It sounded so simple. The body is a wonderful tool in our work because it is always there to remind us; in its various ways it shouts at us, waking us up, taking us out of our dreams and our limiting ideas and so helping to change our attitude.

PAUSING

There is a natural pause between the cessation of one desire and the beginning of the next in which we return to the peace of Heaven. Yet this pause can be covered up as the mind leaps ahead of the body to its next act or thought. But the pause is still there to rest in. If you have not woken up to the awareness of this pause, then introduce one. At any time at all, whenever you remember, stop and be present. Whenever I do this I feel wider, softer and much more loving. For me it is like the magic I experience when relaxing after a yoga practice.

I often like to talk to the teacher training students to discover if anything is getting in the way of their daily yoga practice. One student said apologetically that he had been 'too busy' to practise. This is an

---

18 Sanskrit: *satsang* is a gathering of those who come together to learn about and experience spiritual truth.
19 Sanskrit: in full *samadhi,* deep meditation, the eternal truth of 'not two' is revealed.

example of how our involvement in the transient world can hold us back. Remember you have the choice to make Heaven your priority! It's all there is. It's no good being sorry or apologetic in excusing your ego – just change. If you make your practice your first choice then the 'busyness' feeling will melt away. Give full attention to what you are doing and you will experience the joy of the present moment. As Joseph Campbell[20] would say, 'Follow your bliss'.

HEAVEN ALONE IS

We can all act as mirrors, reflecting and reminding each other of Heaven. To assist us in keeping our mirrors clean we have:

1. Our daily practice
2. The good company of fellow students
3. The inspiring works of the Masters
4. The presence of a Master

It follows quite naturally that when we are engaged in something we love our full attention is there in the moment.

Have you ever felt lifted by being in the presence of someone who is completely absorbed and at-one in their work, or when you are in meditation or in a posture? You feel you could hold it for ever – you even have no idea how long you have held it. This eternal moment can occur at any time and with practice of the above points you will find that it will happen more frequently. You *can* reach perpetual consciousness. It's there waiting for you, calling you to come out of your dream.

---

20 Joseph Campbell (1904-1987) was an American mythologist, writer and lecturer.

AT-ONE-MENT

This word reflects the realisation that God and man are one. It is the union of yoga[21], the *samadhi* expressed by yogis and the Self-Realisation and Advaita taught by philosophers. It is not possible for the mind to comprehend at-one-ment because mind is never at-one; it is always somewhere else, anywhere but in the present moment. The ego mind is made up of opinions, beliefs, theories and conjectures while the Universal Mind is complete *knowing*. To access the Higher Self we need to step over the thinking, chattering brain.

Heaven knows nothing of the finite world. It just is. In times of stress, when the front brain (located behind the forehead) is busy, or when we have a headache, we may make the gesture of clapping a hand to our head. This *mudra*[22] or action usually helps to quieten the head. External pressure on the outside can relieve internal pressure. Iyengar had a method for quietening the front brain: as the student lay in relaxation he would carefully fit the arch of his foot over his or her forehead and transfer his weight onto it. I found it peaceful and effective.

The present moment is all we have. It is where truth and light exist. It is eternally inviting us to come back, to wake up and see clearly again. In the here and now we have the opportunity to be able to drop the prejudices and judgements of past impressions which are accumulated by the ego mind. Love is the way. Love has no conditions, no measure; it is complete acceptance and without prejudice. Love is to join. In love there is no separation; you *become* the love and are at-one, whole and perfect.

An example of being at-one can be discovered through meditation. Our mantra might be anything at all: a posture, a phrase, a sound or

21 Yoga: from the Sanskrit root '*yuj*', meaning union.
22 Sanskrit: *mudra* is a symbolic or ritual gesture practised in Hinduism and Buddhism.

a touch. Through this we may realise and return to One-ness. Actually, we have *never* left it; ego mind only imagines that we have. The only requirement is that we give our full attention, 100%, to the mantra. Were we to give just 1% to the ramblings of the ego mind it would not work. So join with your mantra completely. We know this is true and only need to be reminded of it. In at-one-ment there is no opposite, no duality.

The ego is born in the moment of forgetting and then we begin to think and falsely believe we can plan, do, make progress, possess, rise above or see ourselves as separate and different from others. This is when the trouble begins. It is all an illusion; it is all a dream. It is all in the mind.

Once I dropped an old-fashioned thermometer on a stone floor. The glass broke and the mercury (quicksilver) smashed to the ground and broke into many tiny, perfect silver balls, all sizes and all complete spheres. They rolled about and whenever they neared each other they sped up and merged, forming a larger, perfect sphere until they were combined as before. Similarly, just like the quicksilver, it is our nature to be at-one in harmony, complete and perfect. The separation, the creation, is our illusion but it is created to assist us to realise the truth: we are all one with God. To strengthen this knowledge we need reminders and the manifest world that we have created *is* our reminder. When we are fully realised our transient world will disappear as it is no longer needed.

Your creation is perfect for you just as it is, but you can choose whether to accept it as a classroom or a prison; you can meet every seemingly challenging situation with love and understanding, or criticism and fear. These are the only two ways about it. The classroom can take you to Heaven while your angry or critical reaction will take you into the illusion of a fearful ego world, a prison. Fortunately, like the quicksilver, there is always a natural pull to be unified and whole. By grace, inspiration comes in many forms and at any moment. With a change of attitude you can be free again.

As we have said before, there is a great opportunity to be found in a difficult situation. It is your chance to wake up and look inwards to the source of the challenge – not to blame the world for it. Yet how we like to find some thing or person to blame and pin our discomfort or anger on. Our anger, however, has nothing to do with worldly things. You are never angry for the reason you think. It's not the world's fault. There is nothing wrong with your world. Look inwards at your thoughts; they are the root of your reactions in life.

Take the analogy of a man who visited the cinema for the first time. Not realising that the picture of a roaring, pouncing lion was only a projected image, he took it to be real and ran up to the screen, attacking it. Similarly, once you see the image for what it is, the film or the mind, then there is no fear. That fear will disappear just as when you wake up from a disturbing dream; the whole dream story disappears and you realise that you have been safe in bed, 'at home' (in Heaven), all the time.

FOLLOW YOUR BLISS

It is early spring here in the Cotswolds. Before sitting down to write this I walked into the dew-laden garden. The sun was up, casting a bright, watery light on the lawn and there, under the willow, amidst the vivid green grass, I spotted some violets, single proud little flowers, each showing off their beauty as they pushed themselves up through the earth. I was struck by the contrast of the saturated colours of green and violet in the sunlight and in the stillness of the morning I felt a shiver of energy and delight and a feeling of wanting to share and show it to another person.

But we all find our bliss in different ways. A fellow yoga teacher finds bliss when she is skiing. You can sense it in her voice as she describes skiing off piste in the virgin snow, pure snow that is glistening and sparkling in the overhead sun; she is in Heaven under the clear blue sky. My husband feels blissful when he is listening to a classical concert. In my experience, I received such an awakening, such an uplift of energy during my first class with Iyengar on his annual visit to London that it lasted the whole year until he returned.

What is your greatest pleasure? When are you in Heaven? These moments wake us up. It's as if creation is *asking* us to wake up all the time, offering us beauty, peace, tranquillity and bliss everywhere. Encourage these moments and allow yourself time for pure happiness, whatever lifts your spirits. Being at one with the violets, the sounds, the views or the action releases creative energy and can lift you for long periods. People say 'I still feel in holiday mode' long after they have returned home or 'I feel a lift from my weekly meetings'. The more creative energy that is released, the more becomes available to us. This energy, like the sun's rays, is there all the time, but it can become obscured or clouded over and temporarily forgotten.

If you ask yourself that question, 'What is your greatest pleasure?' and you have to search for the answer, could it be that you are taking life a bit too seriously? And when you do experience pleasure then why not share it with others? This enlarges and magnifies it, not only for the recipient but in yourself. Find bliss in your work, whatever it is. Your clients will recognise your enjoyment in your attitude. You may smile more frequently, be calmer and kinder and as you share your bliss you will find it is quite contagious. Just one person in a room, office or class, working from their heart, can quite change the atmosphere. It's attractive, it's catching and so we all 'suffer' from it!

So let's follow our bliss down the particular avenue we like best and eventually we may realise it is to be found in every single avenue all the time. Have you noticed in these moments that there is no feeling of time passing? The present moment is eternal. When you step back into the present there is no thought of past or future or time – there is just the peace and bliss of now.

DISAPPEARANCE OF THE TRANSIENT WORLD

SAVASANA – CORPSE POSTURE

Daydreams can be very exhausting. 'Wouldn't it be nice to take a holiday and get away from it all?' the ego mind suggests. 'Imagine sunbathing on a beach somewhere.' Yet true rest from mind, body and spirit is to be experienced here and now. One way to prepare us for this is the practice of yoga, where you work to wake up the *tamasic*, sleeping areas in the body and calm down the *rajasic*, over-active parts, thus synchronising mind and body into the present moment.

By giving complete attention to the posture you are in the now. This is what yoga is about, using the body as a tool to bring back a state of *sattva* where the mind no longer travels around but rests in its true home – here – free from transient distractions. It is in this state of yoga or *sattva* that the spirit can shine. It may take a few moments of practice or much longer to come back to it, but if we keep listening to our body we will feel when it is in harmony – in the present – and also when it is time for relaxation, *savasana* (corpse posture).

In *savasana* we lie down on our back, quite straight, with space between our arms and the trunk and between our legs; chin down, palms of the hands turned upwards, feet falling sideways, we let go completely. So, starting with an exhalation, take three deep breaths.

Feel the full support of the floor and allow your body to sink down, even the inner body. With the back of the head heavy now on the floor, widen the space between the eyebrows and allow yourself to be suffused with ease.

Please do not deny yourselves the pleasure of *savasana*. This is complete relaxation. It is the most important posture (remember: posture equals attitude) because it will bring you back to *ananda*, bliss. After fifty years of practice I still feel that bubble of bliss as I open my eyes after *savasana*. It just rises up for no apparent reason and there is an overwhelming desire to share the bliss with others. I feel it is a great privilege to teach; it uncovers joy for the students and the teacher alike.

NEAR-DEATH EXPERIENCE

I received a new knee last week, which was quite a big event as I'd been putting it off since I was in my teens. I've been trying all sorts of other ways to make it work but even Giovanni Maciocia, the great acupuncturist, said he couldn't do anything for me. So I had a change of attitude and went for it.

I spent four days in hospital; it was quite magical really – I pressed a button and someone appeared. It was like being in a five-star hotel. Looking a bit like a ghost in a white sheet, I walked down to the operating theatre, hopped onto the table and asked the anaesthetist to please give me the minimum because I was quite interested in what was going to happen. Unfortunately, he didn't go for that idea and so I asked him brightly if this would be the nearest experience I would have to death. He took a step back. I assume he thought I was questioning his ability to knock me out, whereas the reason I asked him was because Iyengar had once said to me in *savasana*, 'This is the nearest experience you'll have to death'. It only took a few seconds for the anaesthetic to work and really it was quite a heavenly experience. It's difficult to describe, but there were definitely no worries. I felt as if I was sinking into warm black velvet. It quite took away any fear I might have had of death.

I'm not advocating it, but I'd like to share that experience of death with you. There was complete freedom from the transient world and my ego. Without this attachment I was fully present, in fact *sattvic*, with no past or future. I was quite free of any thoughts. It's just a complete experience. It's not even 'me' experiencing it. Everywhere became lighter and brighter and it was so delicious I just merged with it. I believe this moment is available for all of us when the transient world of time and space is no more and you are just *being*, with no physical body, worries or limitations. You are so expansive that you are everywhere. There was no world, no time or space for hours – hours which passed in the blink of an eye.

The next thing I knew was when the surgeon, dressed all in green, was looking down at me on the trolley bed. He was saying, 'No yoga.' I explained I'd been practising for fifty years and had my mat in the corner of the ward, but he suggested I give it a rest for a while.

TRANSFORMATION

A young man on one of our yoga retreats was an expert walking guide in geology, flora and fauna. We were on the Greek island of Lesbos at the time and really it was quite fascinating to see wild families of tortoises, vivid snakes and beautifully coloured tropical fish. Six years previously this young man had been shipwrecked at sea and somehow managed to survive in extremely cold waters. In fact he was the sole survivor. I feel it must have been his will-power to live that kept him alive for so long in such icy waters. He was rescued finally and when he woke up in intensive care and found himself to be still alive he thought, 'I've spent a lot of my life sitting on the fence and holding back, so now I'm just going to go for what I really want to do'. And he did. He was dynamic, spontaneous, interested in everything and great company. His near-death experience had given him new life.

GLIMPSES OF REALITY

Here is a story from Plato's *Republic*[23]: A group of people have spent their lives chained up in a cave, facing a blank wall. They are unaware that there is a flaming fire behind them and that figures are passing in front of it. All the chained group see are shadows of the moving figures projected onto the wall, nothing else, and so they mistake these shadows for reality and begin to give them names. Socrates, who is telling the story, remarks that our perception of the world is exactly like this and we are only liberated to the truth of reality when we ascend to something higher.

Even the figures that cast the shadows are part of the illusion and this trickery of ideas is the barrier to being able to see clearly. We can, though, get glimpses of reality when we join with others to share first-hand truths rather than ego stories. This is good company, whether it be a yoga or philosophical group. We can all recognise the voice of truth when there is no ego or self-aggrandisement present. It's as if the *prana* rises, energy lifts and we speak and respond from the heart.

This state can remain with us. Like our practice it is a reminder that calmness of mind, together with clear vision, is our natural state. It is egoless, where there is no fear, only love. We feel in harmony with the world and there is no separation or difference between people.

23 A Socratic dialogue, written by Plato around 380 BC.

I was once asked to teach yoga to a group of young people with special behavioural needs. I went into their common room to find about thirty or forty teenage boys and girls lounging around in a smoke-filled atmosphere. They didn't take much notice of me standing there, so, raising my voice, I shouted bravely, asking, 'Who wants to do some yoga?' Some of them, still lounging, gave a half-hearted reply so I demonstrated a posture and asked them if they could do it. They gave it a try in an unenthusiastic way, but *very* gradually a few more joined in. At the end of forty minutes I asked who wanted to relax. There was a much better response. Some even got out of their chairs to join in and soon they were all lying higgledy-piggledy on the floor.

As I talked them through the corpse posture there was such a stillness in the room, such a freedom and a vast silence. I looked around at these boys and girls and their faces were relaxed and open; they were so innocent and clear. It could have been a group of professors, train drivers, doctors, gardeners. . . it could have been anybody. Without the ego we are all the same and the spirit shines. I asked them to breathe deeply and stretch and then, as they got up, they began to put their different ego-hats on and so became their characters again; yet for a moment they had been free. They didn't have to pick up their baggage after *savasana* but they did so, unaware that they had the choice to be free of the burdens of the ego.

CHOOSE TO PRACTISE

Unless you are born with the realisation that there is no separation you need to be shown that you do have the choice. By working together we can reflect the truth back to each other, namely the truth we already know in our hearts, that we are indeed all one.

Any stress we experience in our life is related to the pressure of passing time. Yet when we are present in the eternal moment there is no pressure, no passing time. We do indeed have 'all the time in the world'. When we are at-one with what we are doing we can enter a state of meditation where the world stops and disappears. Have you ever been so absorbed in your occupation that you have no idea what time it is? You may even experience such a moment when you are quite still and not doing anything at all.

I remember climbing down my grandparents' stairs when I was five. Stopping on the landing, arrested by a view of the sunset, I became quite still and transfixed. All movement stopped in the clouds and in me. I loved that moment so much that it often flicks back into my mind.

Shantananda Saraswati explains why such a moment is trans-formational: 'Love is the motive force behind all the processes at work in the world to sustain it.'[24] *(Record)* Love is the one true emotion. All the other emotions, like jealousy, hatred and possessiveness, are all born through lack of love. So when a person appears angry or frustrated it's really a cry for help. Try giving love instead of reacting to another's frustration. It can quite dissolve a negative state.

Realise what all the great sages knew and taught, namely that love dissolves fear and that any emotion *other* than love is related to fear. Fear is never in the present. It is imagined. Just allow your love to flow. It is all you have. Of course the ego can play such cunning tricks to keep us away from our true home and that is why we need a discipline to follow. It is from Patanjali, one of those great sages, that we have inherited the well-trodden path of yoga.

Dawn is an especially helpful time to practise, when the earth is just waking up and the sun's rays have a powerful, *sattvic* effect.

24 Ashram talk 29/4/1973.

Sattva is present also at dusk – sunset. There is a natural stillness that comes as the night turns into day and when the day turns into night. It's like the dead point in movement. See the pendulum at the end of its swing as it hangs motionless for a moment in the air before it descends; watch how, in negotiating a high-jump, an athlete will become motionless at the peak of the jump; observe how a ballerina holds the stillness on her points. Just so, feeling the profound stillness on the earth, your *pranayama* and meditations will come easily.

I try to practise at both morning and evening meditative times, but it's your choice. For you it may be appropriate to practise yoga in the morning or before you go to bed. There is always time for that which you value so really it's all a question of priorities. If you find that your yoga practice brings peace of mind and happiness to you then it is surely of great value and if practised first thing in the morning can change the whole tone of your day. I find that the period before the world gets going and while the household is still asleep is an excellent start to my day. If you feel a bit heavy and sleepy first thing then have a wash before beginning your yoga. Drink water, but don't eat before practice as digestion uses your vital energies.

Remember that it doesn't always have to be a work-out. You may like to practise recuperative relaxing postures in the evening before your *pranayama*; meditation leads so naturally from this and can enhance the quality of your sleep.

Patanjali has written extensively on the eight limbs and has explained the *sutras* (texts on Vedic philosophy) for our understanding of yoga. He and other enlightened beings have bequeathed and explained the Vedas for our benefit, but to make it our own experience we do need to be faithful to our daily practice.

'Follow your bliss.'
Joseph Campbell

PLAYFULNESS

*'Unless you change and become like little children, you will
never enter the kingdom of Heaven.'*
Matthew 18:3

CHILDREN AND YOGA

I used to hold a yoga class for young children when we lived in Cheam. The conservatory in our farmhouse was thirteen metres long which was just the right size. Every Wednesday at 4 p.m. children came straight from school to attend the class, my two daughters and my son bringing their friends home with them. I soon discovered that the best way to teach children yoga was to get them to copy me rather than talk them through a posture. The trouble was they were so observant and copied so well that I had to be pretty good. If I didn't straighten my back leg completely in a warrior posture then neither did they.

I didn't challenge the class too much. When demonstrating a tree pose and balancing on one leg, I would ask, 'Can you do this better than me?' They did! If I ever asked them who was the best, every hand would shoot up – and they all wanted to be in the front row. How different they are to adults, whose attitude is often to want to hide and stand at the back of the class.

When youngsters are still growing and their spines are not properly formed it is better neither to physically correct nor to help them up into a posture like head balance. If they are not strong enough to get up themselves then they are not ready to do it. Some children, though, unlike some adults, are quite fearless and will go straight into head balance without thinking about it. They don't stay up for long and can wobble about, but as they are so relaxed and without fear there is no problem there. When I asked one of the little boys in the class to come down, he didn't move. He had got himself up into a head balance against the wall but hadn't yet worked out how to get down!

I found I was able to keep their attention if I worked quickly and didn't hold the postures for long. After three quarters of an hour we relaxed. Most of the girls and some of the boys would sit quite still in lotus position with their eyes closed for three minutes while the rest chose to lie down. Inevitably, there were a few peeps and giggles.

One of the group, Sarah, was eleven and had cerebral palsy. She had difficulty in walking and in her speech, yet she had a very positive attitude and a winning smile. Her mother always brought her to the yoga class, helping her to take off her socks and shoes and change her school clothes for a t-shirt and leggings. Sarah will be in her forties now, but that child's enthusiasm and effort has stayed in my memory because it was so strong. Whenever I gave the class a new posture like a sitting twist, *she* was the one who would try the hardest and get it. Sarah never gave up. She was used to putting 100% effort into everything she did and was so pleased and happy with her achievements. In later years she worked her way to a scholarship at Cambridge and was able to drive an adapted car. Congratulations, Sarah. Wherever you are now, I hope you are still enjoying your yoga.

PLAY TIME

Up to the age of about three or four children are more spontaneously right-brained. In other words, they don't intellectualise. They just *are*. There is no tomorrow or yesterday for them. No past or future. Joseph, my grandson, is six and as bright as a button. He hardly eats anything, but is full of life and understanding. He goes to sleep at 10 p.m. and wakes up in the morning at 5.30. He doesn't conform at school and apparently has dyslexia. Once, when I asked what his favourite class was, he said, 'Play time'. His reading and writing at that point were non-existent and if his teacher asked him to spell a word he would query, 'Do I say what's in my head?'

When we took him out to lunch a few days ago he picked up the menu and ordered some food. What had happened, I asked him, that he could read suddenly? 'I just *think* more, Granny,' he told me, pointing to his head.

Actually, the right brain always leads, even in intellectuals; we then quickly transmit information to the left. The left brain takes over in some cases, but this intellectual centre is much slower than the right brain while the emotional response is even faster. All this of course doesn't imply that we should be childish in our attitude, but simply to be open without prejudice.

Prejudice or pre-judging? I asked Joseph to drink a glass of cabbage water (it looked rather like apple juice). He stared at it before responding with a definite 'No!' I admit it was a tall order, but I continued, 'Just try it, Joseph. It's so good for you.' He screwed up his face and repeated, 'No.' So I said, 'That's prejudice.' He answered, 'I don't want prejudice, I want apple juice.' His mind didn't know about this thing called 'prejudice'. What a gift to be so liberated!

WORK, REST AND PLAY

For harmony in life there needs to be a balance: one third work, one third rest and one third play. Balance is important for us. We all have natural measure; for example, when to go to bed, when to get up, when to eat and how much. You can observe this with a baby, who will definitely let you know when he or she is hungry. An infant will fall asleep when tired and then rather unsociably wake up with a beaming smile at 4 a.m., wanting to play. As the baby starts feeding herself she will push the food away when she's had enough and that's usually it. The mouth stays shut.

Don't forget that as an adult we also possess this natural measure and should listen to our body and its needs. Becoming too serious about *anything* is a warning sign: perhaps you have become too involved or attached to the outcome of an event, to your appearance, your skills or what others may think of you. Take a step back and open out to the moment, feel your feet on the ground, lighten up, be present like a child.

WORK

Can we consider our daily occupational work during the day to be our playtime? It's important not to get too serious or attached to it so try to keep it fun and joyful. I teach yoga for an adventure-travel company whose directors display a generous attitude towards their employees. An allotment is provided where staff can grow vegetables, there is a self-catering kitchen and barbecues after work; they also offer a variety of activities, my yoga class included. The workplace is immaculately clean with bowls of fruit on the desks, each individual is self-employed and they appear to have fun and to work together extremely well. I sense a wonderful atmosphere when I walk into that building and a light, caring attitude passing between the young people.

Spiritual practice, of course, is our real work. So can we make time in the day to read enlightened books and/or to practise our yoga postures, *pranayama* and meditation? All these experiences widen our horizons and serve to release us from worldly attachments.

REST

A deep, dreamless sleep where mind falls quiet and still is total and complete. But if the mind remains active, churning over thoughts, then even though the body is tired it means the duration of sleep can be short. As you sleep, your active mind may dream about all sorts of different things and that is exhausting. After eight hours of this the alarm goes off and you get up. Is it any wonder you feel shattered?

Here are two suggestions that have worked for me: Go to bed before midnight and get up when you wake. If you then decide it's too early you can go back to sleep for a while. Now that's alright if you fall back into a deep, dreamless sleep, but most often the mind returns to its dream world. Just remember that when you first wake up, before thoughts and attachments start, *sattva* predominates. In this fine state the mind is alert, quiet and free, providing you with all the energy you need.

PICNIC TIME

Children know how to play and often their games are quite intricate. Bring back that child-like state of wonderment. A friend who was feeling down in the dumps was diagnosed by a clever Ayurvedic doctor as having 'picnic deprivation'. So let's be child-like and have fun!

'The more one judges, the less one loves.'
Honoré de Balzac

DREAMS

'We are such stuff as dreams are made on.'
The Tempest, Act 4, Sc.1

THROUGH A GLASS DARKLY

When we are identified, fascinated and even besotted with this manifest creation, we believe it to be real. However, there is an important fact which at first may be difficult to understand, but when accepted can change our whole attitude and enable us to realise the truth. The fact is that we ourselves have created our world through our judgements, prejudices and thoughts. We project them onto worldly objects just as we do in our dreams at night and, depending on how we are feeling, we may blame the transient world for our suffering.

Actually, there is nothing to categorise or judge. As it says in Corinthians (1. 13:12): 'For now we see through a glass, darkly; but then face to face: now I know in part; but then shall I know even as also I am known.' So it is that we see our transient world darkly through prejudice, past ideas and labels which we attach to people and things. It's all mind stuff. You see, there is no real world of time and space, only Spirit or God and when this realisation dawns we can see clearly, face-to-face with God.

I am up in Glasgow now, sitting in the bay window of a hotel room, waiting for my nephew's wedding party to arrive. It's September and the leaves are turning early in this beautiful, well-wooded garden. It has been extremely dry and the drizzling rain is welcomed by the thirsty, rusty-red foliage. It is by just sitting here looking out of the window and writing to you as simply and clearly as I can that I am really understanding it; there *is* no separation, just a wondrous picture, a film. My transient thinking fills the screen and I am the source, projecting it out there. It is all just one big projection, this time and space. Such sayings as 'the guiltless mind cannot suffer'[25] make sense to me now. How can you feel guilty when it is all imagined – the whole story, even the suffering? Think of the relief you feel when you wake up from a bad dream and realise it has all been just that, a dream? It's the same. It's all a daydream.

COME OUT OF YOUR DREAMS

Is your mind full of thoughts? Perhaps they are telling a story about how you would like this or that situation or person to be, or about your work or relationships. Can you accept the situation just as it is, without judgement, criticism or wanting to change people or things to suit your ideas? We become so attached to this body of ours, forgetting that to accept things as they are and not wanting to better the situation to suit ourselves is freedom. Bring back the child-like state of wonder, gaze around without attaching your attention on any particular objects. Let your hearing run out to hear all sound as if you were listening to an orchestra. Expand your awareness – let there be no limits.

As we have said earlier, suffering can come when you feel you have been misjudged, hurt or unfairly blamed and you find it difficult to let go of that feeling. It may take some time, but whenever you

25 From *A Course in Miracles*.

observe a nagging thought, forgive and let it go. It's only a mind story after all. Don't give up. With practice you will find you become free again.

There is a story about two monks that illustrates how we can create a burden for ourselves by holding on to an idea. The monks, James and John, were out walking when they encountered a young woman crying by the river bank. She told them that she needed to get across, but the water was too deep; deciding to help her, James took her on his back and carried her to the other side. John followed after. When James had set her down on dry land the monks walked on, but four miles later John said, 'You are a monk and you shouldn't have carried a beautiful woman on your back'. James replied, 'But I put her down four miles ago, John. Isn't it about time you put her down too?'

We all suffer from our attachments. As I was travelling into London on the M4 the other day my attention was drawn to the lines of illuminated advertising hoardings, some as high as houses. I was attracted by the image of a particularly good-looking man advertising after-shave (although he still had stubble). I wished I could look at him for longer as we drove on. How strange, I thought, that I should attach my awareness to an illuminated advert. And then, looking around me, I thought – goodness, I'm attached to everything I see!

Is it always like this, or is it perhaps different when you find yourself lost somewhere and are looking at things as if for the first time? You search for a familiar landmark and then, when you finally recognise it, you stop this detached looking and the knowledge or set of ideas about it crowds in. It's the same on holiday when you look at a scene for the first time, really observing it before the prejudices, the ideas and judgements and even the labelling come in. When we are looking through all these preconceived ideas about familiar objects, how much are we *really* seeing? Is it actually our judgements and limitations that we see? This is looking with the body's eyes, creating our own world and reacting to it. Everything in this creation, the thoughts and the bodies, are all a reflection of our mind; we are the authors of our dreams, not just at night but in the daytime too.

When we realise that we invent these stories, these manifestations of our thinking, we can begin to understand why we work to clear the mind and quieten the chatter. And when we do choose to do this, a miracle happens. We step into Heaven and out of our self-made separate world. In Heaven all is one. There are no clouds to look through; you see brightly and clearly as the real you is freed from your judgements and thoughts of separation.

What stops us from being permanently in our true home of Heaven? We have become so attached to our separate, self-made universe that it has become our choice. We love it more than God's world. Just remember Jesus's words: 'Thou shalt love the Lord thy God with all thy heart, and with all thy soul, and with all thy mind. This is the first and greatest commandment.' (Matthew 22: 37-38)

When we remind ourselves every day that we love God more than anything else and that He is our first priority, then we return home to God's world. This influences the way we experience life. We can work so hard in the material world to try to better it, creating craven images which we worship, but in Heaven there is nothing lacking. There is only love. No insurance policies or deadlocks are needed here.

A fellow philosopher travelling to India noticed that the Dalai Lama had boarded and gone onto the top deck of the aircraft into first class. On the flight, being a bold young man with plenty of drive, he decided to walk up to first class and, as luck would have it, there was a spare seat in front of the Dalai Lama. So he knelt on the seat, looked over the back of it and asked the Dalai Lama how he could lead a better life. The Dalai Lama smiled and simply said, '*Whatever you do, do it to the best of your ability*'. Wise words.

Your attention is everything. Be wholehearted and focus your concentration on whatever is in front of you. When you choose to give full attention to the matter in hand you will be living in the present and not in a dream.

IMAGINATION

Our hopes and yearnings can lure us into the world of imagination where our conjured-up thoughts and stories seem to take on a reality. Here's an example: You go to the railway station to meet a friend but the train doesn't turn up; you wait on the platform and you wait. Questions start to run through your head . . . What if the train has crashed and caused a horrific accident? Has my friend been taken to hospital and if so, which one? How will I get to visit? I should take arnica with me because that will help the shock. And so the story continues. There is, though, an alternative. As you wait for your friend's train to arrive, simply sit on the platform and enjoy watching the world go by. After all, there's no such thing as waiting, just being. Enjoy the moment!

There is, of course, nothing really wrong with thoughts; it's only when we cease to observe them and believe them to be real that we lose ourselves in a dream world. Shakespeare's Hamlet debated this when he asked that famous question: 'To be or not to be . . .' Whether it is to know you are an actor playing your part on the world's stage, or 'not to be', in other words to take this transient world, the actor's script, as real.

Are you perhaps taking life too seriously and identifying with the part you play? If this strikes a chord with you then give priority to your spiritual practices. And if you catch yourself being carried away by a dream then remember the *Rasa Lila*[26] – we are here to play. Remember to give all your attention to whatever you are doing. There is no half and half. You are either here or you are not. So-called problems, whether they be physical, mental or spiritual, are all in the world of mind. Be free of your dream world and play your part well.

26 Krishna's Divine Play, the Cosmic Dance, which embraces reality and illusion.

APPRENTICE TO A MASTER

NO THINKING

On one of my visits to see Iyengar in Pune I left my two small girls with my husband's parents for three weeks. This was quite a challenge for me as I had never been parted from them before; the grandparents, of course, were looking forward to caring for the children very much. My head, though, was full of ideas about how the girls might be feeling lonely and missing me as much as I missed them. They were fine as it happened, really enjoying staying with their grandparents in a lovely cottage in the country.

Over in India, my 'Intensive' with Iyengar was certainly that; in fact it was the most challenging experience I've ever taken on. There was no time to sightsee or shop – we had two classes a day, morning and afternoon, with the time and duration never fixed; that's how it goes in India. The class could be two or four hours long. Iyengar was a law unto himself. Every instruction was direct, vital and alive. He wanted your full attention and would never entertain the mind wandering off. There was nothing intellectual about his instructions either; they were practical and what he taught was absorbed by the posture in your body and not in your head. 'No thinking!' he would shout, nor were you allowed to stop and take notes in class. When we asked him for philosophy classes he declined, saying yoga was an *experience* not an intellectual pursuit for storing up knowledge for later. When he was instructing, words of wisdom would drop like pearls, precise and apt. There was no time to think or doubt. True knowledge comes from observation and there is very little thinking to do in yoga, if at all.

We are such intellectuals in the West, often adopting a posture where the head (intellectual centre) protrudes forwards and the hips (physical centre) are drawn back. Ideally, when standing in balance, your ear, shoulder, hip and ankle should be in line.

If you ask 'Is it going to rain today?' would you consult the weather forecast on your mobile rather than look at the sky? When you complain of backache how often does a doctor look at your back? When children are instructed to 'think first' they can lose the spontaneity of the moment. Iyengar's strict and precise discipline paid off. We worked wholeheartedly with full attention. Once, I drifted off for a moment when he was demonstrating and before I noticed he was behind me. I felt a cuff on my head as he woke me up with a shout of, 'Dull mind! Where were you?'

In the standing postures Iyengar was quick to notice I had a dropped right shoulder. 'Pinch in the bottom inner corner of your shoulder blade,' he would instruct. 'Roll your collar bones towards your ears and lift the breastbones vertically up.' If, during the class my collar bones rolled down, he would shout with feigned anger, 'You're not doing it!'

When I left England I had aching feet and was wearing arch supports and metatarsal pads. In class, Iyengar gave me a torrent of instructions: 'Raise the three middle toes, push down the outer edges of your feet in front of the heels, press down the first metatarsals, then the fifth, the inner and the outer heels, lift the inner ankle bones . . . I did not say the big toes. Make an arch like a rainbow.' On and on it went until I felt my feet would drop off with tiredness. Yet after this amazing experience they were made better and I returned home without needing supports or pads.

In my own practice at home I could never work to that same degree in strengthening my feet, try as I might. When being taught by a Master and being open to his instruction it has the effect of bypassing the conscious mind with all its limitations and ideas, in this case my feelings about my feet. They had a history of operations and treatments and these ideas were holding me back, limiting my full capability. We are fortunate indeed to be in the presence of enlightened teachers like B.K.S. Iyengar, those sages who enable us to be free of the burden of history and past memories.

KNOWLEDGE

After a class with Iyengar I would note down his observations and instructions. They were perfect at the time and went straight to my heart, waking me up. For years I carried these notes around with me to my teaching residentials, having the idea that I would give them back in a class but, whereas in a different time and a different place the instructions had been perfect for me, those particular moments had now passed. The instructions never quite applied to, or suited my students. I didn't need to save up these wise words for later. True knowledge or instructions come from clear seeing in that moment. When teacher and student are present and receptive then knowledge will arise. It is important to voice this true knowledge. Ignorance exists in the world because wise men do not speak.

It is my experience that when working as an apprentice to a Master there is an osmotic exchange of knowledge. I experienced the pleasure of being physically corrected by Iyengar; the correction bypassed the intellect, the body woke up and absorbed its instruction and so the next time I practised the posture the correction happened. The body had remembered Iyengar's touch.

It's a privilege to be with a Master craftsperson, whatever their trade; just to stand and watch is an uplifting experience. The transference of knowledge is a gift, quite different to the knowledge acquired from study where you read and make notes and pass exams. When a Master is 100% open to sharing his or her years of experience and practice, the apprentice takes a quantum jump and so can absorb that expertise.

We benefit so much from the knowledge bequeathed to us by the sages. To absorb this wisdom we need to fall quiet in the mind, be humble and open and accept the gifts offered. When Iyengar gave an instruction in a class he would not take kindly to explanations or justifications as to why you could not get into the posture. He would not listen to ego excuses but would praise the most unlikely students for their great endeavours and 100% efforts. Physical ability does not come into it. It is your attitude, your wholehearted endeavour that matters. If you think you can, you can.

PAST, PRESENT AND FUTURE

SUFFERING IS IMAGINARY

This morning, before I began teaching a yoga group, one of the students informed me she would be 'taking it easy today' as she was going to visit her son in prison after the class. She happens to be a strong yogi and is capable of holding the postures for a good length of time, but today she kept coming out of them early and resting.

This is an example of the kind of trick our ego mind can play in order to gain thinking time. In yoga, when you are giving your full attention to the posture and are at one with it, it's impossible to think because your attention is focussed only on that posture. I pointed out to this particular student that she was capable of holding for much longer and it would be better for her to keep her full focus on what she was doing now rather than entertaining imaginings about how her son was suffering and not being well cared for.

Our strength lies in the present. You are in equilibrium and in your balanced centre when, standing, you keep the right side of the body over the right foot and the left side over the left foot, but when the mind goes forward into the future or hangs back in the past then so does your body. You lose that equilibrium, the strength of the present.

The ego mind is exhausting. That student had to make the choice between either coming out of her future imaginings and turning her full attention to what she was doing now or to allow her focus to wander into her dream state. Happily, she chose to allow the imagined dream to dissolve away, giving full concentration instead to the posture, so freeing herself from the suffering thoughts. I sincerely feel that this will give her strength and enable her to give her son her full attention when she visits him.

FREEDOM

A recent flight home from Australia proved interesting. When we stopped over at Dubai airport, an unaccompanied teenage girl sitting next to me started to cry. Concerned, I asked her if I could do anything to help and after gentle questioning she told me she was upset because she had just heard that the singer, David Bowie, had died. This young woman was suffering from an imagined loss, an attachment, not realising that actually she lacked nothing. So we talked about how well she was being looked after by the air hostess and gradually she calmed down and dried her eyes. Whatever the situation, we should remember that all our suffering is imaginary and the way out of it is to come back to the now.

When we left Dubai and were on the airbus en route to Heathrow, I noticed that four Muslim girls, wearing hijabs, had joined the journey and were sitting in front of me. As soon as the seat belt sign was extinguished they went to the lavatory and returned without their hijabs, their shining dark hair now exposed. They were smiling broadly and as they tossed their heads and kept running their hands through their hair their feeling of happiness was palpable. It was a joy to watch them chattering away excitedly. They had liberated themselves from a restriction and were free. Later, when the plane was beginning to circle around Heathrow, they went off and put their hijabs back on again but they did not lose their smiles or their enjoyment.

We all have a desire to be free, free from restrictions, ideas and traditions, traditions that are so ingrained in our consciousness we don't always realise that we actually are free. Restrictions are all in our minds. In the book, *The Man Who Wanted To Meet God*, Shantananda Saraswati tells a story to illustrate just that: A *dhobi*, or washerman, used donkeys to carry his heavy loads. One day, feeling unwell, he asked his son to load the donkeys with the washing and take them to the river. But when the boy had loaded them and tried to move them he found they wouldn't budge. Noticing that they weren't tied up he went to his father and told him about the problem. 'Ah,' his father said, 'I should have explained that every evening I touch their feet as if I am binding them with a rope and every morning I touch them again as if I am untying them.' So the boy went off and touched the donkeys' feet. Thinking they were now free, they moved and began to walk to the river.

Ask yourself the question, 'What am I compromising in my life?' The ego's chatter in the mind is all false but is also very clever because it is the ego that is imagining that you are restricted. And here's another question to ask yourself: 'What makes me happy?' If you know, then let it happen. No holds barred. Just be aware that the ego mind will bring up excuses and constraints to try to stop you. I don't mean by this that we have a licence to disobey society's laws; we should still observe the *yamas*, the first two limbs of the Eight-fold Path that make up the ethical disciplines of yoga.

PEACE OF MIND

When our limiting ideas are released it is then that the peace of the present moment is revealed in the silence. Once, on holiday in Rome, I visited the Sistine Chapel, marvelling at the ceiling with its inspiring works of Michelangelo. I noticed that about every two minutes, when the admiring murmurs of the crowd rose up and echoed around the small space, reaching a crescendo, a chaplain would hiss a warning, 'Shush!' Silence then reigned for a while, a silence so profound that we all felt it.

HOW TO BE CARE-FREE

What a pleasure it is to watch small children play. Quite unconcerned about what others think and completely innocent of past or future, their minds and bodies are synchronised in the present moment. There is no time, no tomorrow or yesterday for them, only the game as it is happening now.

My husband and I used to enjoy watching our children play when they were very small. It was usually before their bedtime when we were feeling exhausted and they were still full of beans! Despite our comment to each other that 'They *must* be tired now' they certainly didn't show it and I have to say that even our weariness didn't spoil our delight at watching their unpredictable, aimless play. Is that pleasure of ours derived from a memory of how we used to be – carefree – and yet could be again?

A child might be happy one moment and crying their eyes out the next. Also, they may show dislike if reprimanded, but all this is over in a flash as their attention is diverted to whatever is in front of them, to what is happening now. They don't bear a grudge. A grudge or a feeling of resentment is a barrier to our happiness.

The key for us is to be present. There is still a tribe of people in Brazil, the Pirahã, who are said to speak only in the present tense – what freedom that must bring. Imagine if you had no past at all; how would you feel? It could be rather scary at first to think that all your hard work, earning money for your precious possessions, your qualifications, your treasured memories and your personal identification are gone.

EGOLESS MOMENTS

A fellow philosopher friend, Kate, had a virus which knocked her out. She was taken into hospital with a high temperature and didn't seem to know where she was. After two weeks she began to recover, her temperature went down and she looked much brighter, but she still retained a complete blank about the past. She had no memory of it, yet she was quite 'with it' and very much in the present. She was super-aware, loving and fearless. In fact that waking up to the present had freed her from the past and as such she was delightful company.

After four or five weeks her memory returned but her state of awareness and wakefulness stayed. She was extremely popular with the yoga students who questioned her about what it was like to be in the now. She was indeed excellent company.

Perhaps the absence of all this past head stuff might enable us to feel like a small child, free to fully enjoy the present. There are moments – are there not? – when the past falls away and you are in 'the power of now', when free of the burden of the past you can feel light, quiet, harmonious and loving, with no pressure of passing time; time-less, in fact.

Kate developed a brain tumour in later years. She didn't suffer from any pain but found it difficult to speak. Although she couldn't voice her words clearly, she could sing them and this is because the vocal chords are rough in speech, while in singing they are straight. This gradually became worse, until she lost her speech altogether. She could hear and understand well, but had to write messages which made communication slow. In time she lost the power to write and eventually to sit up, yet she remained cheerful throughout. After her death, which was quite peaceful, her husband explained to me that she had been in a state of bliss as the thinking part of her mind had been knocked out. He understood that she was already in Heaven and so he did not suffer either.

Just as in Kate's case when, because of her virus, her thinking mind no longer operated, egoless moments can arise and we come into the present moment. This often happens through necessity as I discovered one afternoon. My four-year old daughter, Christina, was playing happily on a swing in my next door neighbour's garden while I was sitting in ours. An imposing six-foot high wooden fence divided the two. Suddenly, Christina's murmurs of delight changed into piercing screams and I knew something serious must have happened. The sound of her cries fired me with energy, so much so that somehow I was over that fence in a flash. She was clinging to the ropes of her swing, unable to jump off because each time she swung forwards the neighbour's Alsatian dog was biting at her leg. I scooped her up in no time, comforting her as I took her back through the garden gate. In my mind it was now impossible for me to climb that six-foot fence. Miracles happen.

OBSERVING OURSELVES

'True knowledge is in observation.'
B.K.S. Iyengar

MIRRORS

When faced with adversity it helps to be positive and expect the best possible outcome, the most successful result. The universe will always respond. You have created your world with your own thoughts, influenced by whatever subject you choose. How you *think* the world works, that is how it *will* work. Here's a little story to illuminate this:

In a small remote village there was an abandoned house. One day, a puppy looking for shelter from the sun managed to enter it. He approached a semi-open door and on slowly entering a room soon realised that there were 1000 more dogs watching as he watched them. The dog began to wag its tail and prick its ears. The 1000 dogs did the same. He smiled happily and barked at them; 1000 dogs also smiled and barked happily with him. When he left the room he thought, 'What a nice place that is. I'll come more often to visit.'

Later, another stray puppy came to the same place and entered the same room. Unlike the first one, he felt threatened when he noticed the 1000 dogs watching him. He started barking aggressively and 1000 dogs did the same. The dog left the room and thought, 'What a horrid place that is. I'll never go there again.' Now on the front of the house there was a sign saying, 'The House of a 1000 Mirrors'.

All the faces you see in the world are mirrors. You are not responsible for the face you have been given, but you are responsible for the face you make. You decide which face you will carry inside yourself and that will be the one you will show to the world. Remember that the most beautiful things you see are a reflection of what is felt in your heart.

Smile and the world smiles with you, cry and you cry alone. It is our function to keep our mirrors clean and polished so that when we catch a smile we can smile back cleanly without any sarcastic smudges or disbelieving smuts. When you are talking with someone and you catch their smile you know they are present and so the communication flows. On the other hand, if you see misery and sadness in their face how do you respond? Do you frown back, or do you respond with a positive remark and give a lifting smile? Obviously you don't want to beam widely if someone has just had bad news, but you could transmit compassion and just listen.

MIND AND BODY

Eileen, my friend and secretary, once broke her lower leg. She was put into a heavy plaster which immobilised her foot and gave her a most distorted walk. The plaster came off after two months but the walk didn't improve. She had caught the habit and still walked with distortion. She asked for help and when I looked I found there was so much to correct. She could never have taken that many corrections on board so I asked her instead to imagine walking as if the other leg was now in the same sort of plaster. Her body pretended beautifully, with no piecemeal or intellectual corrections needed – just a childlike mimic. For a while she limped with the good leg and then it all evened out and she walked straight again.

Our bodies want to be straight and balanced and will always work towards doing just that. It is our thinking that distorts us. So it is my function when teaching to allow students to think well of themselves and to believe their bodies can move into the posture; once they envisage and think themselves into the posture the miracle happens and they can.

Entertain your visions of how you would wish things and relationships to happen. No fears or doubts. Imagine yourself straight and strong, walking tall.

RELUCTANCE

As mind and body are inextricably linked we could see further into ourselves by looking at the weaknesses in our bodies. When I put this to my yoga students, however, I found it was unpopular.

One of the students, a seamstress, offered me her draper's mirrors (there were three of them, full-length, with the two end ones placed at an angle so you could see a reflection of your back view as well as your front). I gladly accepted her offer and placed the mirrors at one end of the yoga hall in order that the students could observe themselves in action. The result was rather disappointing – the students retreated to the other end of the hall!

A similar reaction happened on a yoga weekend when I took a video camera to the class, thinking the students would benefit from observing their back and side views in order to correct their postures. I was wrong. I showed the video after lunch but no one turned up to see it. Not one!

All this reluctance is because of our egos. We don't like looking at our faults or even admitting that we have them – and yet to work on our weak links is the way to strengthen the chain, both in mind and body.

We have a long landing in our old house with a full length mirror at one end. When I suggested to my eighty-year old mother, who had just had a hip replacement, that she walked towards the mirror to see how she could change her gait, she refused. She had been a physiotherapist all her working life, coaxing patients to do just that, but she could not look at *herself*.

I felt decidedly uncomfortable when I viewed my first attempt to make a practice video, 'Stress Buster', for the students. It showed my lazy legs and that I was practising without a *mula bandha*.[27] I knew I would have to do the whole thing again. The second attempt, with a mirror positioned by the lens, enabled me to correct as I went along. It was a good teacher; it reflected what was needed and allowed me to correct.

REFLECTIONS

We act as mirrors for each other and can learn by these sorts of reflections. Have you ever caught sight of yourself in a mirror and not recognised that it is you? For a moment you are detached from your image of yourself, from your story, your past, and you find that you are looking at this mirror image afresh as if it were someone else. That is before you straighten up or cheer up and start looking as you feel you want to look. Children, of course, can show great detachment when looking at themselves in wonky mirrors, laughing at their distorted figures. So when is it that our attachments and serious side come in? Oh dear, we say, another grey hair or wrinkle!

This book is not about changing your life – it's about changing your *mind* about your life. You could spend your life building a house on the sand in the material world, but it wouldn't last as everything in the ego world, body-mind and all things, is transient. Similarly, if

27 The root lock in yoga.

your *asana* practice was as much as six to eight hours a day you would probably end up with a beautifully strong, supple body but one that would eventually return to 'dust and ashes'. On the other hand, if you used your *asana* practice to prepare mind and body for your spiritual practices, enabling you to be free from distractions or discomforts, you would then be 'building your house' on a rock, as Spirit is eternal.

We need two wings to fly – one in the material world and one in Spirit. If you favour only one wing you will go round and round in circles, or be like an absent-minded professor, brilliant intellectually but with his clothes in tatters and suffering from neglect of the body. So use both wings and fly high. Enjoy your creation and play your part well. *Whatever* you do, do it wholeheartedly. You can enjoy building sand castles in the transient world while knowing all the while that your true spiritual home is built on rocks and that your treasure is in Heaven.

'Love flies on its own wings and knows no laws.'
Francis Lucille

A LEAP OF FAITH

THE EGO VOICE

Who is the boss – ego or Higher Self? We can spend our lives taking orders from the voice inside our heads, running here, there and everywhere. It's as Sri Nisargadatta Maharaj once said – most actions are unnecessary and some are positively destructive. So don't be bossed around by the ego voice. Instead, rest back into the silence and take direction from the Higher Self.

It's all very gentle. Be easy on yourself and don't criticise. To accept things just as they are and not to wish them otherwise is the way to freedom. Expect nothing, even from your nearest and dearest. This may seem like a strong request but remember that they can't read your thoughts so they won't always respond in the way you think they ought to. There's an amusing little saying that goes 'If you think you're realised, then go home to the family for a week or two'. Yet the truth is that if you believe you *can* practise acceptance then it *will* come about.

PAIN

When I stand in front of a class to teach yoga I see a lot of able bodies; any restrictions only appear in the minds of the students. Mind stuff is run on fear and our bodies can hold and trap this fear from past memories of hurt. Pain is not only present in the physical world. Sometimes, when I demonstrate a posture and then ask the students to do it I can almost see the ideas going through their minds – 'I *can't* do that!' – and yet their physical bodies are quite capable of it. So you could call it 'will-power' yoga.

If someone is upset let your heart be open to them and to the purity behind their thoughts. Give that purity the attention rather than identifying with their pain, emotional or physical. By making remarks such as 'You look so *exhausted*', or 'Oh, what a *terrible* operation you've had', it might encourage the person to burst into tears and cry, 'Yes, yes'.

FEAR

In some situations fear of what might happen to you can take over. I have experienced this at times; for example, before a parachute jump, when standing on a high board in a swimming pool or when I was about to make a bungee jump. Approaching the take-off platform, high up on the cliffs in New Zealand, the fear was so great that I couldn't loosen my grip on my helper who was trying to fasten my halter. I shuffled towards the edge of the platform, pulling him towards it too. The worst of it was that my husband, who had climbed up with me to this dizzy height, was saying, 'I *really* don't think this is one of your best ideas. In fact, it's not a good idea at all'.

The fear of what might happen to us is so great and yet it is all taken away as we come into the moment; the freedom when we take that leap of faith is unbounded. Lao Tzu expresses it thus: 'What the caterpillar calls the end of the world, the rest of the world calls a butterfly.'

A thought came into my mind just before I jumped. 'OK,' it said, 'I'm going to die.' Yet my pride wouldn't let me climb back down the stairs so I jumped – and felt like a butterfly! Time stood still. I felt suspended and completely free and unlimited. And for a week afterwards I was living in a state with no fear.

In his poem, 'The Dream That Must Be Interpreted', Rumi[28] says:

'This place is a dream.
Only a sleeper considers it real.
Then death comes like dawn,
and you wake up laughing
at what you thought was your grief.'

I assure you it's a wonderful place to be. No worries, no pressure of time. I felt very joyful in that leap. So what is lacking that prevents us from being in this state of freedom all the time? Is it a lack of commitment?

ONE HUNDRED PERCENT

When you are wholeheartedly committed to something you experience more energy and confidence. There is a great difference between 99% and 100% and it's not just that small 1%. There is a *world* of difference in it. Procrastination, when you hold back 1%, is extremely tiring, yet when our energy and attitude are focussed we don't make mistakes.

I was once privileged to be invited to observe an open heart operation at Great Ormond Street Hospital for Children. Donning the green gown and hat and covering my shoes, I entered the operating theatre expectantly. All was quiet. The theatre team was 100% focussed on a little child's body. The five-year old girl was quite still and yet I noticed that her heart, which was exposed, was beating so strongly and with such force as if to demonstrate how alive it was.

---

28 Jalāl ad-Dīn Muhammad Rūmī was a 13th century Persian poet, Sufi mystic and scholar.

I was encompassed in an atmosphere of loving attention – 100%. Those of us in the theatre were completely as one. Silence pervaded, broken only when the surgeon's kindly voice was requesting an instrument. I felt part of it all, unemotional and clear. After an unmeasured time (it could have been two hours or ten minutes) it was all over and the tiny chest, which had been held wide open, was being closed with stitches. I glanced at the little girl's face. She was deathly white. Her head was turned to the side, with a tube in the nose. My emotions flooded, my body went weak and my eyes filled. I was lost in my story and no longer 100% focussed.

Yet when we are at-one with what is in front of us there is no problem and when we wholeheartedly love what we are doing we are so much more efficient. Try it and see.

UNITY

COMMUNICATION

Our function is to reflect the truth for each other. There is no other way really for we all reflect the same God. Whenever we perform the Indian salute or greeting, *namaste*[29], we are recognising and honouring the Higher Self in each other. It also acts as a reminder for us all, reinforcing our unity.

Our latest granddaughter, Amber, aged eighteen months, came to stay last week. She is very keen to communicate but has only three words in her vocabulary: 'Oh', 'no' and 'purple'. She saw how focussed her parents were when talking on the phone and was desperate to join in. She grabbed the television remote control, glued it to her ear and adopted a serious expression, head to one side. Then she toddled up and down the room in an effort to communicate and speak her three words and 'blah-blah' sounds with great enthusiasm and attention. She stopped every few moments and waited. I answered her through the DVD remote control which fitted the bill perfectly. Amber was so delighted with her line of communication that she would not release her 'phone'; even after half an hour of sounds she clung on, crying bitterly if I tried to take it away.

The same frustration can arise in us when we feel we are not being listened to or understood and cannot express our thoughts and feelings.

29 From the Nepalese and Hindi languages.

INTUITION

Do we rely on smart phones rather than our intuition? Do we set our alarm clock to wake us up rather than using our minds? If we rely too much on technology our natural instinct could become weakened. I took a short cut while driving to the swimming pool this morning and came out of a country lane onto the A44 (my sense of direction is not that great). I didn't recognise the stretch of road and was in a dilemma wondering which way to turn for the pool. I began to imagine how it would be if I turned right and then how it would be if I turned left. This was no help at all so I gave up and fell quiet. A *knowing* came in seconds. I had not worked it out in my head. I turned right and there was the pool around the corner.

How often have you rung an old friend and they pick up and say, 'I was just about to ring you!'? These things happen, so why should we be surprised by the behaviour of other creatures? Dolphins and whales have great communication and even appear to understand our emotional state when we swim with them. It is surely because we all share the same subconscious mind, these gracious beings included. When the busy mind shuts up there is no need for communication techniques. All is known and though Oneness is indescribable we all recognise it and try in our different ways to return to complete unity. The politician may think of Utopia as the perfect state, with equal rights and with everyone having enough food and a home; the yoga teacher might think of holding the perfect posture for ever; a parent will wish her children to be perfectly behaved and brilliantly intelligent, while for a doctor it is having 100% perfect health for every patient. For others unity is searched for in endless sex or food, or in desperately trying to obtain perfection in the material world.

A SENSE OF LACK

At times we can all feel a sense of lack in our lives, perhaps if we are separated from family and friends. We may feel lonely or unloved. We attach emotions like this to a situation, but is it not really simply a longing to be back in a state of unity where there is no sense of lack? Those kind of feelings arise in our ego mind when we have lost sight of the Oneness and perfection of the Universal Mind.

See if you can catch yourself blaming or making scapegoats out of 'things'. Remember that the external situation is never at fault. The world is as it is and our feelings or sufferings are all in our minds. All that needs to happen to experience *ananda*, bliss, is to shut up or, to put it more politely, to quieten the fluctuations of the mind.

I felt I had a 'right' to be worried this week when my excellent help and friend in the office suddenly upped and left due to personal problems. As I walked across the courtyard in a disconsolate way, eyes downcast, a pink rose in full blossom leaned over and hit me on the forehead. It was so luscious and smelt so heavenly that it stopped me in my tracks and that's when the miracle happened. My world changed instantly. I was surrounded by beauty. I saw the lamb in the field, the tits feeding their young in the nesting box and the wisteria, heavy with purple blossoms, draped over the garden fence. It was as if nature and the surroundings were pulling me out of my thoughts.

The world only seems fearful when we drift out of the now and imagine things are going awry. We have choice in every moment – whether to live in the heavenly world which exists in love, or the ego world which exists on fear. When, by grace, we wake up and choose the heavenly world then all suffering is released. The imagination of the past and future drop away and there is nothing at all that we could add to this present moment.

'A thankful heart is not only the greatest virtue,
but the parent of all other virtues.'
Cicero

LOVE, PRAISE AND GRATITUDE

LOVE

Love is one of the most frequently used words in this book. It answers the age old question: 'Who am I?' In the presence of love, emotions such as greed, jealousy, hate, envy and guilt are not possible. If we ask ourselves the question, 'What makes me feel these emotions?' it will be something to do with our world of imagination.

Love is your essence, your true nature, and once these feelings are seen to be something you have conjured up in your mind, then they can fall away. Yet if you are still worried about your feelings, just ask yourself if the worry is true – are you sure that it's *really* true? Observation will expose the untruth.

You don't have to entertain worrying thoughts: let them go! Talking about your grievances and gaining sympathy from someone only adds fuel to the fire. In fact it makes those thoughts appear all the more real. So let them go. Come back to love and they're gone.

We are pure, whole and innocent. From about the age of two the ego begins to form, though it can happen later or sometimes not at all. With this comes the arising of emotions other than love and then guilt can enter, accompanied by the feeling that we lack something. As we grow we forget that we are always at one with our perfect Higher Self. We begin to think that we *need* more when in truth we have all the love we need – in fact we *are* love. It is as Christ said: 'Consider the lilies of the field, how they grow; they toil not, neither do they spin; and yet I say unto you, that even Solomon in all his glory was not arrayed like one of these.'(Matthew 6: 28-29). Those lilies don't need an ego.

When I came out of a three-week retreat what hit me the hardest were all the advertising hoardings. Their general message was that we need this or that product to change us for the better . . . physically, socially and emotionally. How we can be led astray by all this in-your-face advertising.

After a practice or a retreat your mind can quieten down and in this silent space there is nothing you want or need; in your right mind all is well with your world. Perhaps, though, we can be thankful that our mind conjures up 'obstacles' because they are a method of learning. We can learn by observing our reactions, but if we react unconsciously to them we are deep 'in the story' and it feels real. So we need a life, a body, an ego and world experiences; otherwise there would be no way of realising Heaven. So-called obstacles or challenges reflect what is going on in our ego mind. They are our lessons enabling us to see the play.

We can become so attached to worldly things that our ego thoughts dominate and we feel we are lacking and forget that what we really want is to be at home with God. As soon as our priorities are other than God they become, as it says in Exodus, our 'craven images' and the Higher Self is forgotten. We would do well to remember Nisargadatta's words when he said, 'You want what you don't have and don't want what you already have, and so you suffer'. We really do have everything; we are complete and all is well.

The following is from a letter that was at first purported to have been written by Einstein to his daughter, though this has proved not to be the case. However, I think the content speaks for itself and is worth including:

'There is an extremely powerful force that, so far, science has not found a formal explanation to. It is a force that includes and governs all others, and is even behind any phenomenon operating in the universe and has not yet been identified by us. This universal force is Love.

When scientists looked for a unified theory of the universe they forgot the most powerful unseen force. Love is Light that enlightens those who give and receive it. Love is gravity because it makes some people feel attracted to others. Love is power because it multiplies the best we have and allows humanity not to be extinguished in their blind selfishness. Love unfolds and reveals. For love we live and die. Love is God and God is Love.

This force explains everything and gives meaning to life. This is the variable that we have ignored for too long, maybe because we are afraid of love because it is the only energy in the universe that man has not learned to drive at will.

Love is the most powerful force there is. It is the energy to heal the world as it has no limits.

After the failure of humanity in the use and control of the other forces of the universe that have turned against us, it is urgent that we nourish ourselves with another kind of energy.

If we want our species to survive, if we are to find meaning in life, if we want to save the world and every sentient being that inhabits it, love is the one and only answer.

Perhaps we are not yet ready to make a bomb of love, a device powerful enough to entirely destroy the hate, selfishness and greed that devastate the planet.

However, each individual carries within them a small but powerful generator of love whose energy is waiting to be released. When we learn to give and receive this universal energy we will have affirmed that love conquers *all, is able to transcend everything and anything, because love is the quintessence of life.' (Anonymous)*

PRAISE

My secretary in the office was arranging a yoga retreat in India and sorting out suitable flights with least waiting times at airports. This was quite a challenge as the students were coming from all over the place and needed to meet at Kerala airport. I didn't help by suggesting Malaysia Airlines and Air India when she had almost confirmed Emirates. Realising she had started to feel frustrated and was showing anger, I praised her for all the good work she was doing on our behalf, assuring her how this trip would never get off the ground without her clear-minded experience. Soon her attitude changed. All stress dropped away and her voice softened as she said lovingly, 'But I was only worried by the thought of you being stuck in some airport over the other side of the world and me not able to do anything about it'.

As in this example, truthful praise can affect our attitude, our world. Those few words of praise took my secretary back from her head to her heart. The miracle happened and though often a miracle might seem like just a little incident, yet it has the same effect as something mind-blowingly important. We would do well to show our praise, gratitude and love as often as we can. Adopt the habit. Praise lifts you as much as the recipient. Would you have the strength to see and voice praise in the midst of an argument with someone? Letting love in can turn the tables on the situation and allow the miracle to happen; then both of you would come back into your hearts, each realising in that moment that your meaning is the same and that there is nothing to quarrel about at all.

GRATITUDE

My daughter, Karuna[30], lives in Australia and when I was in hospital receiving a new hip she showed great love and care by ringing me up all the time. This was heartlifting for me; the pain I was experiencing quite disappeared while talking with her. These calls, though, came at strangely inconvenient times: when talking to the surgeon, on a bedpan, or in the middle of the night. A few weeks after the operation I rang her to say how very grateful I was that she had shown such loving kindness at that time and how much it had meant to me. That lifted us both.

Another example of gratitude occurred in a busy restaurant. A waiter, who was working flat out, looked surprised when I said, 'How are you?' It stopped him for a moment. He'd been serving for eight hours, he said, and no one had asked him that. Just before leaving I thanked him profusely for such a lovely meal and he gave me a really wide smile. It is so important for you to acknowledge – to actively show – the good in others by giving thanks. As it says in *A Course in Miracles*: 'You but give it to yourself.' Again, it lifts both the recipient and the one expressing the gratitude.

30 *Karuna* is the Sanskrit word for loving kindness.

*'It is not the magnitude of our actions but the amount of love
that is put into them that matters.'*
Mother Teresa

WIDENING OUR HORIZONS

YOGA STUDENTS

Recently, eleven trainee yoga teachers attended a weekend that I was running in London. They were all attentive and open, yet quiet and wakeful too, working together as a group and assisting and helping each other; because of this I found that I could hold them for longer and take them further into a posture than before. The group's trust and love took each of them through their imagined limits into their peripheral, wider movements which are very rarely used, if at all. This was easy with the two new students who, being unfamiliar with the postures, had no preconceived ideas about how far they could go and how long they thought they would last out.

We remember pain; it can be held in the body as a fear and so we form safety nets or blocks. We imagine that restricting our movements will protect us from the anticipated pain while instead they limit us and hold us back unnecessarily. The pain is in the past and the body is fine right now. So now is *always* alright.

After that weekend I was delighted to receive emails from the two new students and from the second year students too. The gratitude they expressed told me a great deal about them and their attitude towards the teaching. In an atmosphere of trust and care they had been able to widen their horizons, move through their fears – their limitations – and go further into the postures. This is what yoga is about, working with full attention, seeing through our self-made limits and stepping into the unknown – finding the space to go further. When the restrictions fall away there is a freedom, a lift of energies, a little burst of joy and awakening. I felt lifted by their acknowledgements. It was they who achieved, not me!

Love is not love until you give it away and sharing is important. Similarly, it is a gift for teachers to give away and share their knowledge. Not only is it a real pleasure when your students take on the corrections you have given them but it also confirms and strengthens your teaching. How delighted is a Master craftsperson when his or her student shows promise and absorbs their wisdom.

On another weekend yoga retreat one of the teacher training students was helping to make lunch and so missed the instruction on what particular *asanas* would be appropriate for a student who was extremely stressed, this being the series of postures that would calm down the anxiety and bring the student back into balance. The trainee asked if the instruction could be repeated but was asked instead to copy the notes from another trainee teacher. This student, after the class, had made copious notes on the subject but was unwilling to share them when asked, not realising that to share and go over what she had noted would also benefit herself and consolidate her knowledge.

Claim nothing. Give away. Ignorance arises in the world when the wise do not tell.

LETHARGY

Do you ever experience that heavy *tamasic* feeling that you are stuck? A student once asked me, 'What is lethargy?' Well, here's an example: It's a Sunday afternoon and the sun is shining. The idea pops into my head that I really should cut back the hedges in the garden. It's a great time to get out the shears and start clipping. Instead, I sink into a comfortable chair and say to myself, 'It's just for ten minutes and besides, I need a rest after lunch. What's on the news?' In no time at all my energy changes. I'm locked into my chair with a heavy body that doesn't want to move. I should have gone with the spontaneous impetus to go out and cut that hedge – all the energy I needed would have been there, but lethargy set in instead.

When an inspiring idea comes in and you act on it and go with the flow of energy it's easy; your mind is clear and you commit to the idea – it's then that something happens. The universe goes with you and allows it. On the other hand, if you choose to sit on the fence the mind will quickly jump in and dissuade you from acting in the now. Negative thoughts appear: 'I can do that later . . . there's no time now . . . if I help that elderly lady she'll want to talk for ages . . .' All these thoughts take you into the world of imagination.

Some yoga students who initially feel motivated to take the teachers' training course may feel differently when they get home. Fear can set in, swamping that first, inspiring thought. 'I really can't enrol on the course,' they tell themselves. 'I can't get away . . . the children won't manage without me . . . the house will get messy and there'll be piles of washing up and laundry waiting for my return . . .' etc., etc. In truth, all may be well, with children happy and cared for by family or close friends.

If you are ever in doubt then go with your first thought, the one before the *ifs* and *buts* and *cannots* flood in. Instead of weighing up one decision against another, trying to work it out, go with the inspiration and when that arises there will simultaneously be a lift in energies to carry the action through. Don't allow a lethargic thought to bind, limit and drain you.

'All friendly feelings for others are an extension of man's feelings for himself.'
Aristotle

OUR HEART'S DESIRE

SHINE THE LIGHT

Seduced by the ego's dreams of wealth, prosperity and greatness, we create problems and stress. We work so hard for these castles in the sky – wonderful houses, designer clothes, being in a position of power, etc. – and such thoughts dominate our mind and become our gods. Yet is this what we really want? We should take the first commandment on board: 'Thou shalt love the Lord, thy God, with all thy heart, with all thy soul and with all thy might.' When we really know and love and are at-one with the God within then there is no stress.

When we create a so-called problem we can actually use it as a tool to undo the imagined difficulty. Look straight into it, not evading or side-stepping the dilemma or thinking 'I'm too busy right now'. Face it fair and square and keep looking. We need to see the fear and anger and expose it in order to uncover the love within us. Remember the love is always there, just covered up by our ego world. Expose the love. The reluctance to do so may be understood by these words of Marianne Williamson[31]: '... Our deepest fear is not that we are inadequate. Our deepest fear is that we are powerful beyond measure. It is our light, not our darkness that most frightens us.' Why should it be difficult to shine the light to express 'I love you'? Do we think

31 Marianne Williamson is an American spiritual teacher, author and lecturer.

it is too extreme, that others may laugh or think us insincere? These thoughts come from our ego and are never quite the case.

When discussing the heart chakra[32] I notice students are reluctant to go straight to the heart and find it difficult to refer to or mention love, talking all around the word without actually saying it. When I asked one girl, 'Do you mean love?' she answered in a relieved voice, 'Yes. Thank you'. It is an all-powerful word and works miracles.

ESSENCE

Consciousness knows nothing. Our essence, our Oneness or God within us and without us *knows* absolutely nothing. It's a clean slate, quite clear of limitations. It is nothing to do with the world of matter, facts and figures. They are all in our minds, our thoughts. They are our created images.

Here's an analogy: A contraption hangs in our sitting room window. It's a clear crystal, suspended on a short chain from a minute solar panel. When the sun hits it the heat provides just enough energy to rotate the crystal. As it rotates, the facets of the crystal reflect the colours of the flowers in the garden – the purple buddleia, the pink and red roses and the blue of the sky behind them. A rainbow of colours reflected by the crystal dances around the room. Fascinated by the movement and the beauty of this play of creation, I attach labels and descriptions to the dancing fairy colours. Yet that's just mind stuff; an interpretive story. The crystal is quite transparent, pure and whole. In essence it remains unaffected. It just reflects what is in front of it without being changed in any way. That pure crystal is like an empty space within our hearts, free from all thoughts, yet limitless. It feels good to rest there a while.

---

32 There are seven chakras, or centres of spiritual energy, in the body. The heart chakra is the fourth. When the heart chakra is open one is filled with love and compassion.

Whatever is now is perfect. Don't long for tomorrow rather than today or prefer the past to the present. Pooh Bear understood it: 'What day is it?' asked Winnie the Pooh. 'It's today,' squeaked Piglet. 'My favourite day,' said Pooh.

Our hearts open when we obey the first and greatest commandment, which is to love God, and when this happens the head automatically quietens down and we return to Heaven. Here there is no conflict, no untruth, just a sense of knowing.

A student on one of my yoga teacher training courses is a barrister; he told us that when he is defending in court he always knows whether the accused person is telling the truth or not by the sound of their voice. Similarly, we all have the ability in our hearts to know and recognise the truth, so if a dilemma arises in your mind, just fall quiet and sense the truth.

Imagine living a life of love where every interaction is without fear, where there is only divinity wherever you look. There would be no deliberating voice in the head, pondering that 'If I did this so-and-so would happen, but if I did that then this would happen'. It's all nonsense. Living in love there would be no decision making. Remember there can be no choice to make in your Higher Self, for all is one.

A DISCIPLINED MIND [33]

It is my experience that people gathering together in a group to share truths need a discipline to keep their direction towards the spiritual light constant. In my teens I was fortunate enough to join a group of kindly, yet serious philosophers. I had arrived in London as a photographic student and was staying in a hostel in Gower Street. My room mate and I began to look for an evening class to join. The

---

33 See also the Appendix for a full description of the ancient teaching of *Sanatan Dharma*, a moral code explained by Shantananda Saraswati.

choice was philosophy or French. As I have dyslexia and struggle with language I was heavily in favour of philosophy, so off we went on a London bus to the School of Economic Science in Suffolk Street.

We left that first meeting full of energy and laughter, but it was only much later that I came to understand what had happened to make us feel so happy. It was because the tutors and helpers there were carrying out the school 'rules' which they expressed quite naturally. This was their discipline:

- give full attention when communicating with another person
- give no second-hand examples, but only personal experiences when illustrating the material being read
- do not speak about a third party unless they are present
- encourage students to put into practice what they have understood from the material
- work for the work itself and not for personal gain
- be punctual
- speak the truth and act accordingly

These disciplines will be in place quite naturally when we put the truth (or God) first in everything we do. Discipline is necessary for spiritual growth and the acceptance of this brings freedom of mind; the ego gives up and you are comfortably present and purposeful. No fears or doubts can squeeze in, for with these disciplines the mind quietens down and we can hear again the omniscient silence.

Give your practice precedence. Practising first thing when you awake can change the flavour of your day. You may be surprised at what talents you have. We need a disciplined mind to experience a spiritual awakening to the truth. We are then able to choose for the light in every situation and experience Heaven on earth. This realisation is not acquired on one's own, but by working with and for others; it is being able to see a reflection of ourselves through them.

NO LIMITS

ATTITUDE

I had travelled to Kerala in India and as I stepped off the plane into the warm night air I felt relaxed and comfortable; even though I had come to run a two-week yoga retreat it was as if nothing was expected of me. I felt free.

It was easy to rise at dawn and take yoga, *pranayama* and meditation with the group. When talking with the locals my experience was that they have all the time in the world: no anxiety, no rush, no pressure of time. When looking into their still, dark eyes I sensed that they were born with the knowledge, the truth that this moment is the only one we have. Their presence and connection with their Higher Self was evident. Their attitude was so contagious that the group of twelve yogis, most of them training to be teachers, all caught it. We lived in a bubble of happiness.

In the afternoons, when it was too hot to practise yoga, we would enjoy Ayurvedic treatments; these included hot pads of herbs massaged into the back; oil trickled onto the forehead and body; milk baths and massages given with the feet. We received so much from these treatments that, suffused with joy, we gave it back to each other. The conversation at meal times was full of praise and happiness.

Often, on our retreat evenings, Dawn, a fine yoga teacher, would play her gong for us. Five-foot in diameter, it's a solid brass instrument called Kheiron. When I asked how she had come to choose this particular gong – she seemed so at-one with it – she explained that actually it was the reverse: the instrument had chosen her. She had had a different pitched gong in her mind but when she tried Kheiron she knew this was the one she wanted to play.

Interestingly, in ancient Greek mythology, Kheiron was a wounded centaur warrior, a god who healed others to heal himself. So it is with yoga. It is easier to see others' challenges but not so easy to be aware of your own; in this way, yoga teachers teach what they need to practise and so learn themselves. Teaching is healing and every one of the student teachers that I have taught had a personal challenge they needed to work on. Whether we realise it or not, by teaching and working for others we are working and healing ourselves.

From India we travelled to Australia. I noticed that when teaching a yoga class of Australians they displayed a positive, healthy, 'up-front' attitude. They stood square and tall, and some of them were indeed *very* tall. They had beautiful feet with straight toes and a level of fitness way above ours in Britain. It might be because of the climate, but they have a most positive attitude, with many of them preferring to spend their evenings walking by the ocean than watching television. I found them to be open-hearted people and easy to teach.

ACCEPTANCE

Acceptance brings freedom: freedom from the desire to somehow change the situation you are in. As we have said before, this notion of how you would like to change your world never works out because the ideas will be from the past or future and you are trying to bring them into the present. When we accept the world just as it is we can relax and when we let go of the idea in mind the body relaxes too. Tensions in the body arise from ideas of past or future. Wake up the body, bring it back to life; be at home.

When practising yoga be present and give your complete attention to the posture. This will bring you out of your daydreams. Whatever you give your attention to gives life. The discipline of stretching to your maximum brings awareness; the skin is directly connected with the brain and as we stretch we wake up and our attention is brought back. Stretch your hands open. Now stretch a little further and it's that little bit extra, more than you usually stretch, that is the yoga of it; it takes you out of your habitual pattern and expands your horizons. You are in the unknown where there are no limits but great possibilities. By doing this you have freed your mind. Your greatest ally is your body. It will show you how you are. There is no problem with the body; it's the thinking that's the problem.

An example of this concerns a friend of mine. Living in an ancient house with lots of stairs, she believes her arthritis is preventing her from climbing them. Even before she tries, she appears to be convinced that she can't get up the stairs, expressing her aches and fears while clinging on to the handrail. A change of attitude could help, whereas if I sympathised and suggested that she needs a chairlift it would make her story true. Her mind-set is that it can only get worse.

OBSERVE

Observe and see, not with the body's eye but with your inner eye, your intuition. Body and mind work together and particular yoga postures will influence certain centres in the body or chakras. Your intuitive centre, the *ajna*, which lies just below the centre of your forehead and into the head itself, is linked to *vrksasana*, or tree posture. The more you fall quiet and trust your intuition the further you will see. It takes practice and most of us are out of this practice. Give it your attention and be still and the answer will come.

When you sincerely ask for help it *always* comes, though it may not be in the form you expect. It could come as an inspiring thought, you might hear or read words that answer your question, or a person turns up to help you.

Jill Bolte Taylor[34], a brain specialist, observed herself having a stroke that was occurring in the left hemisphere of her brain. (Remember that the left brain is the rational, analytical, speech and reasoning side.) When she realised that this left side was knocked out and that only her right brain was operating she was, as she put it, 'in la-la land', or in Spirit, not in the body. She also discovered that she couldn't dial for help because the numbers on the telephone pad didn't make any sense to her. Luckily, the left brain began to come back in waves and she was eventually able to make the phone call; however, when contact was made, the voice at the other end sounded like a Golden Retriever and so too did her own voice! She managed to get help at last and now she lectures, giving her audience clear observations as to what actually happens when you lose the material world and enter Heaven. We can, of course, all choose to be there, though we do need the left brain to survive in the world.

GO WITH THE TRUTH

As soon as you accept and make the decision or take the direction that comes from inner stillness, then the mind can focus. Understand that you can never make a 'wrong' choice. Take the action of flipping a coin when you are searching for an answer to something. Even as that coin leaves your fingers you know what you want the answer to be; so just go with what you know regardless of how the coin falls. Accept what is. When the mind stills, the answer comes. Follow it and go with the truth.

34 See Ms. Taylor's book, *My Stroke of Insight*. Her website is www.drjilltaylor.com

APPENDIX
INSPIRATIONAL TEACHINGS

B.K.S. IYENGAR (14/12/1918 – 20/8/2014)

O n the day of Iyengar's death I felt that it was both a great celebration of his life but also a liberation, for he had been given a challenging body to look after and nurture. I remembered one occasion during our practice – he was forty years old at the time – when he put my hand on his lumbar spine and then went into *trikonasana* (triangle pose). There was a strong, grating feeling. That made me understand his strength and his ability not to be affected by the pain. He once said in a class, 'Teachers never complain of pain', and he never did.

After the death of his teacher, Krishnamacharya, Iyengar contracted jaundice where even the whites of his eyes were yellow but he kept on teaching us. He had a weakness for coffee and would drink a cup straight after a class. My idea of coffee was that it was there to wake you up and give a temporary energy lift. Heaven knows Iyengar did not need that! He was always abounding in super-energy.

I first met him in the early 1960s when, as a teenager and experiencing acute back problems, I was fortunate enough to 'fall at the feet' of the great Master. He was holding classes in London at the time, sometimes with as few as twelve students, and it was through his teachings that he showed me how to work to be free of pain. His forte was alignment in postures. He taught us, his students, how to physically correct, waking each of us up through his deft touch. He never wasted words: his commands were precise and direct . . . 'Lift your left kidney' . . . 'Roll your collar bones up' . . . or tapping a limb, he would remark, 'Lazy'. His English was sometimes interesting to unravel: 'Make your foot like a rainbow.'

Suffering from tuberculosis and a curvature of the spine, Iyengar began his studies in yoga as a teenager, under the guidance of Tirumalai Krishnamacharya. He took it up as a personal challenge, excelling in *asana*. He also became a master of *pranayama*, with his inhalation and exhalation each lasting two minutes.

Iyengar came to London in the late 1960s, giving a demonstration at the Methodist Central Hall, Westminster. The place was bursting at the seams. I remember he came hopping onto the stage in 'crocodile' (with his body off the ground and parallel to it, he maintained his balance using tiptoes and hands).

Yet through all this strictness, Iyengar had a great sense of humour; his voice was loud and penetrating and his belly laugh equally so. He would feign anger at a student and then wink at the audience. In class, he would never ignore a needed correction and was the most hardworking person I have ever known.

Not long after our early meeting I followed Iyengar to Pune, India, where I studied to become one of his senior teachers. This involved taking his teacher training classes and assessing students for their certificates. Having started by training just three women, Iyengar's teachings have spread today across the globe. He is described as the father of yoga and has bequeathed to the world a wealth of excellent yoga teachers.

A fierce picture of B.K.S. appeared in *The Times'* obituary column, with words highlighting his initials: 'Bang, Kick, Slap'. Now I must have had more classes with him than most and have *never* seen him hurt anyone. He would, though, hit out at egos and poke fun at our egotistical ways. For example, I have been called a 'vulture' as I seemed to be the first on the scene to hear his observations when he was demonstrating finer points. Another time he reprimanded me when I was correcting a student under his eagle eye with, 'You just want to be a super star'. And another time he said, 'I will take away your teaching certificate'. This was when he gave me an elderly lady to correct. She had pearls everywhere – necklace, ears and fingers. And even worse, she would not take off her nylon stockings. When Iyengar came round to me, to see how the corrections were going, she was slipping all over the place on the wooden floor!

Iyengar never said 'good' to me in all the fifty years I have been his student, but then who wants a teacher who says 'good'? That might just puff up your ego.

From all the tributes sent into *The Times* they picked out the most dramatic. It's my experience that newspapers prefer drama to truth. Is this what we want to read? One week later this appeared in *The Guardian* by a fellow student, Silvia Prescott[35], and it gives a much truer picture:

---

35 Silvia Prescott, one of Iyengar's first British students, died on 3rd November, 2016

'I first met Mr Iyengar in London in the summer of 1971. That's what we all called him then, before the name 'Guruji' became fashionable. I had been learning Iyengar yoga for nearly a year, and practising every day, but when I met him that was it. I realised he was a spiritual teacher as well as a physical one.

At the time I was teaching keep-fit classes, which was odd because I was the butt of everybody's jokes in gym at school. But I had a friend who was in this class and she begged me to join. So I went, and it turned out to be a very good form of keep fit, systematic and sensible. And that started me off on physical things I'd never been able to cope with before, when I was in my 40s.

Yoga at that time was becoming very popular. There was a programme on television about it, and a friend of a friend told me I must try it. She said there was an ILEA (Inner London Education Authority) teacher training class starting. Silva Mehta was one of Mr Iyengar's few students in the UK at that time, and she was asked by the ILEA to train yoga teachers. I started doing the class in 1970, in a class of around 25, and I met Mr Iyengar when he came over the following year, during the hot season in Pune.

After that he came every summer. I didn't find him intimidating. Some people did, but I found him inspiring. There's a clip in a forthcoming film about him in which he says, 'See how many students I have in spite of my wild nature?' He did have a wild nature; he was quick, and could be sharp, but I never felt it was a personal thing – it was always so you could understand better what you were doing. I've seen teachers in other fields who have got cross or irritated when people didn't understand. I felt he could just get a bit impatient if you couldn't get it, and there was a tremendous affection for everybody, and for the subject, and that outweighed everything else. There was never any doubt in my mind that I was going to go on with yoga.

Once in those first few years he went to Bristol and gave a public talk, and my parents went to hear it. There were questions at the end, and someone asked, 'Why do you practise yoga?' Mr Iyengar thought for a few moments and then said, 'Because I want to make a good death'. That made such an impression on my father, who was then in his 80s. He had such a positive attitude.

I didn't go to Pune for the opening of the Iyengar Institute in 1976 because my mother was dying, but I went the following winter, and then most years after that – probably around 20 times in all, for around a month each time. Those trips became part of who I was. Before I went I tried to imagine India, and I pictured mud huts. Then, of course, we arrived in Bombay, and getting out of the plane was just amazing. The heat came at one like a wall, and the smell of smoke, because we arrived early in the morning and everyone had little fires, all the workers in the airport and so on. And there were skyscrapers! Mehta, our teacher, was with us. She had a friend with a flat in a skyscraper with a beautiful view overlooking the sea. We arrived at the weekend, and Mr Iyengar used to teach classes in Bombay on Saturday and Sunday, so we went to the classes and then took the train with him back to Pune.

We had a room with six or eight beds and a bathroom, a worktop, a sink and a little grill. Upstairs was the yoga hall. Mr Iyengar taught a class every day, for two or three hours. Sometimes there would be an asana (poses) class in the morning and then a pranayama (breathing) class in the late afternoon, or a separate class for sitting poses or forward bends. There would be local classes going on at the same time, and Geeta or Prashant (Iyengar's daughter and son) might be teaching those, but he would very often be there. Right up to this year or last, he was often in the asana hall while classes were going on, doing his own practice. Very often somebody else would be teaching and he would interrupt, and say: 'Don't do it that way, do it this way.'

Sometimes we went on trips to see the caves and did a bit of sightseeing; we went to Bombay for the weekend and did the classes there and saw friends and had tea in a hotel.

Classes were always different depending on the class, on him, and on the weather. Sometimes he might have decided to do something but then change his mind. In the first couple of years it was more intimate because there were fewer people, but even then it wasn't 'tell me about your life and what's worrying you'. I felt he knew what he had to give, and that there was really no point in getting into anything that might interfere with that. I never felt I wanted anything other than what was being given.

Being corrected in a pose by him was totally different from being corrected by anyone else. I can still feel what his touch was like, and it was just magic. Sometimes people who didn't know him, or people who like gentle, easy yoga – you know, do something for three minutes and then lie down and have a rest – said Mr Iyengar was horrible and that he hit people. It's true he might give somebody a slap, but that slap would wake up that part of the body so you didn't forget it. He was extraordinary, a genius; there's no doubt about it. But his teaching was not for everyone. Different students need different teachers and different teachers find different students. It's very strange and fascinating.

It's hard to define his contribution to yoga. People often identify it as the use of props – things that can help you understand how the body works, and it connects with the mind – the belts, blocks and ropes he used in classes. That is certainly something he did in a big way, but it's not the only thing. The important thing about the aids – the supports that help one get the posture – is that when one gets into the right posture, or something closer to it, something happens to the body that has an effect on the mind, and that's the alignment and the balancing of different parts of oneself. It's what he was, not what he did, and it's more a spiritual and psychological matter than a logical one. As he got older he talked and wrote more about spirituality, but he never did to begin with. 'Light on Yoga' was 90% physical. The spiritual side was implicit.

Recently I was looking at a bit of film in which he is adjusting somebody in a headstand, with ropes around their legs. In 90% of people the leg is not in correct alignment – the foot, the shin, the knee and thigh are not aligned correctly, which of course can lead to damage. In the film Mr Iyengar was teaching an assistant how to tie wooden rods into the ropes so they pushed this student's shin bones in such a way that she understood she needed to turn her kneecap out.

But it's not all logical or rational. Sometimes when I started teaching yoga, I found that my hand would go to touch somebody in a particular place, but I wouldn't know why. He had that sense to the nth degree. I occasionally got a little flicker of it and I'm sure most people who practise and teach Iyengar yoga get something of it, too. I think he inculcated it into people in some way, but it's very hard to put into words.

Not everyone in that first group I was part of went on to work as an Iyengar yoga teacher. Some students invented their own yoga – that's a great trick, to invent your own yoga! Some people imitated Mr Iyengar and are still imitating him to this day, and some people didn't know how or why, but they just did it. That's what happened to me, and I know other yoga teachers who are the same. It's not a question of learning how to teach, but of understanding what you're doing.'

It is a gift that Silvia shared the flavour of Iyengar's teachings so eloquently with us all. For those that were fortunate in having classes with him and also those who received his teachings second and third hand – the magic is still there. It was as if he had x-ray eyes and, understanding how your inner body was functioning, gave you the appropriate posture to balance you. I will be forever grateful to B.K.S. Iyengar, my teacher and friend.

PATANJALI'S EIGHT-FOLD PATH OF YOGA

The first two limbs, *yama* and *niyama*, are the great commandments transcending creed, country, age and time. There are five individual disciplines in *yama:*

- Non-violence *(ahimsa)* – this concerns loving, which adhered to gives freedom from fear and anger.
- Truth *(satya)* – Gandhi said, 'Truth is God and God is Truth'.
- Non-stealing *(asteya)* – taking that which is not yours. It doesn't necessarily have to be material. It could be stealing the silence.
- Self-restraint *(brahmacharya)* – spiritual study of self restraint; practising sexual restraint; not being promiscuous.
- Non-hoarding *(aparigraha)* – taking only what is necessary now.

There are also five individual disciplines in *niyama:*

- Purity *(shaucha)* – this means body and mind are not entertaining impure thoughts.
- Contentment *(santosha)* – accepting the present moment.
- Wholehearted effort *(tapas)* – burning off any impediments; not entertaining any hindrances or restrictions.
- Spiritual study *(svadhyaya)* – entertaining or referring to one's Higher Self.
- Dedicate your actions and will to the Higher Self/God *(Isvara pranidhana)* – not looking for personal gain or results but working for the love of it and not for reward.

The third limb is *asana* – practice of the postures/attitude. The postures train and discipline the mind, bringing steadiness, health and lightness of limb, agility, balance, endurance and great vitality.

The fourth limb is *pranayama* – science of the breath. Although it is practised during *asana*, it is advisable to be free of physical discomfort through practising *asana* before sitting for *pranayama* or meditation. As lions, elephants and tigers are tamed very cautiously and slowly, it is advisable to do the same in *pranayama* practice. It strengthens the respiratory system, soothes the nerves and helps to reduce craving. It takes a long time to master slow, deep, steady breathing. Master this before more complicated techniques.

The fifth limb is *pratyahara* – withdrawal of the senses from the objects of sense. It is to be neither distracted nor absorbed by this transitory world, keeping your attention on what you are doing. It doesn't mean closing down your senses, just don't be pulled out by objects or thoughts.

The sixth limb is *dharana* – bringing the mind to one-pointed attention.

The seventh limb is *dhyana* – meditation. Being at-one.

The eighth limb is *samadhi* – the blissful state of unity, transcending time and space.

If you were to practise one limb perfectly the other seven limbs would be present, including *samadhi*. Every limb is to quieten the mind so that we can realise we are at-one and that there is no separation and that we are already in Heaven.

Given this choice, wouldn't we all choose Heaven? What gets in the way? Is it thoughts, our favourite ones that pull us out of the present and into our dreams? To assist us to stay present we have these eight limbs of yoga and perhaps the most commonly practised is meditation. To bring the mind out of our illusory state we focus on a mantra. This can be a sound, a candle-flame, or diagrams such as a mandala. Giving your complete attention to your mantra, being at-one with it, draws you back from your dreaming.

To be given a personal mantra is a precious gift which you keep to yourself. It can be used at any time. Having focussed on your mantra you may rest back in stillness and when you are aware of thoughts coming in, repeat it. Don't fight with the thoughts, just gently bring your attention back to the mantra. It's like finding your way through a crowd of people – you don't push them out of the way or resent them, you look for the spaces in-between. Go for the space. Mind the gap!

SANATAN DHARMA

As humans we are here to learn and we need guidance and direction. *Sanatan Dharma*, the ancient Vedic text, holds the Truth. Advaita, or non-duality, is at the heart of every great religion, but through the ages, in their setting down, the scriptures have been changed. I am not talking here about Christianity. I'm talking about what Jesus, the Buddha, Adi Shankara and other enlightened teachers actually spoke. All the enlightened Masters spoke this one truth and we would do well to study the philosophy of *Sanatan Dharma*.

As His Holiness Shantananda Saraswati, Shankaracharya of northern India, explained: 'Sanatan Dharma is not bound by space and time, or division of the human race at all. It is for the human race as a whole. All religions are supported on the basic idea of *Sanatan Dharma.*'

Its basic concept has been summed up in ten principles and these have been translated from the teachings of the Shankara:

1. Have confidence and patience. If there is no confidence, there can't be patience. These two are united and individuals should develop them together.

2. Have tolerance and forgiveness. This means having consideration, and giving pardon and being tolerant of all the difficulties and awkwardness and faults of others, so that you provide them with space, and in due course, when they see there is no reaction, they may learn something better which you hold very dear to yourself.

3. Have self-control. The senses are very fast, and if the mind is turbulent, receiving impressions from different sources, it is quite probable that sensual hunger and thirst may be inflamed because of the beautiful things being seen in the world. So every individual needs to have some control over their sensory appetite and expressions.

4. Take only what you deserve and consider everyone else equally deserving. So, do not take anything extra because all that you accumulate extra is theft. You steal from the universe and you deprive other people. Do not keep anything more than your share.

5. Be pure of body and mind. One has to learn to clean one's body, one's mind and one's heart, and for that one has to find a system through a teacher.

6. Moderation in all things. There is a natural course of the use of the senses, and those can be regulated. The rules are prescribed in every tradition, and from these one has to learn how to use one's senses within those limitations. One does not curb the use of the senses but regulates them. The curbing of excessive use will then take place naturally.

7. Have discriminating intelligence. Our minds are capable of discrimination or reason, and we are expected to use our intellect and find out the causes of things and use them as necessity may arise.

8. Search for knowledge. One has to acquire true knowledge.

9. Be truthful. There is only one truth about an aspect, there can't be two different truths about the same subject. So truth is important, not only for people in a highly developed and cultured society; the need is everywhere, but somehow people like to serve their own ends through their own concept of truth.

10. Be free from anger. One should never get agitated under any circumstances. There may be occasions when a hard line is very necessary, usually for the sake of education, but taking a hard line is not necessarily getting agitated. One can tell the difference between righteous agitation or wrong agitation. If one is wrongly agitated one cannot take right action, so this has to be avoided.

THE ISHAYAS

How it happened

My husband, John, and I used to meet up with Ken and Angela, two friends who were meditators like us. We had been in a philosophy school for years (philosophy here meaning 'the love of truth'). Angela, a beautiful woman, had been suffering from psoriasis since childhood. She had tried many remedies but to no avail. On one occasion, noticing that the psoriasis on her arms had disappeared completely, I asked how it had happened. By way of explanation she said she had met some monks from the Ishaya tradition and was so impressed with their attitude that she and her husband had decided to be initiated into their way of meditating.

Well, it must be powerful, I thought, if it can help to heal Angela's psoriasis. We asked if we could meet the Ishayas and learn more about their philosophy and so we did. At the time, the monks, six young men and women, were living in a rented house in Hendon. They certainly had presence, seeming unhurried, light and free. The Ishayas always give their full attention when talking with you; there is never a feeling that they have something else to do. In listening to you they never react in a judgemental or critical way and when this happens I feel a sense of freedom too. Freedom to be who I really am.

Two of the group, Narain and Maia, offered to initiate John and me into their way of meditating and we soon became good friends. They accepted our invitation to join us on our yearly yoga retreat on the Greek island of Lesbos and to be our guest philosophy tutors. The students loved their company, too, and we all Ascended with them (the Ishayas' Ascension is a simple meditation process based on techniques called 'attitudes'). When we returned home and were teaching our usual weekly yoga classes the other students wanted to know what we had been doing on our Greek island as they said there was something different about us. So Narain came and gave talks to them and held weekends in our home and yoga centre in Cheam, Surrey. He also continued to join us in Lesbos and has been giving us talks ever since.

A few years after we had been initiated, Narain and Maia went their different ways to continue the Ishaya teaching, but I always kept in touch with them. We were delighted when I got a message in 2002 saying they were coming back to live in London. I happened to mention on the phone that I didn't think Maia's name suited her and Narain said, 'Yesterday, the Maharishi[36] changed it to Satta[37]!' I also knew that one day Narain and Satta would marry.

Moving to the Cotswolds

John is a shoemaker, manager of John Lobb in St James's Street, Piccadilly. In 2002 he took semi-retirement and this meant we were then free to move away from our home in Cheam, London to greener fields. I had been longing for that day. Our eldest daughter had moved to the Cotswolds, to Chipping Norton, which was very near to North Leigh where I was brought up and so we agreed to join them and share a house.

We found a suitable building called Lane House Farm, a 14th century old house situated in Shipton-under-Wychwood, a small and beautiful village just six miles from Chipping Norton. Our plans for sharing the property had to change, however, when we discovered it was a listed building and would not easily divide. My daughter and her family decided then to look for their own, smaller house and John and I did the same. In the process, we happened to bump into

36 Maharishi Krishnananda Ishaya, current leader of the Ishayas. More information about the Ishaya Foundation can be found at www.thebrightpath.com
37 Adapted from the Sanskrit: *Maya* meaning illusion and *satya* meaning truth.

our original estate agent who queried why we hadn't bought the 14th century farmhouse. When I explained that we couldn't afford it on our own, she said, 'Oh, but the owner really wanted to sell to you!' Discussing it between ourselves we admitted that we had fallen in love with the place – there was such a harmonious and happy feeling about it – and so we made a smaller offer which, much to our surprise and delight, was accepted. I wrote and told Narain that we were pleased they were returning to London but that we now had the opportunity to make the long-awaited move to the country.

Our new location

Lane House Farm (LHF) was similar in some respects to Church Farm House (CFH), our 16th century home in Cheam. Both have several bedrooms, old fireplaces in every room, crowds of chimney pots and even an underground passage that leads to the adjacent church. There is also a village hall nearby and a pub.

As with CFH, we were faced with the same dilemma for our new home, namely 'How can we afford to live in such a house?' Previously, we had divided CFH into five flats which we let, keeping the main house for us and our three children. Now though it was just John and me. How, we sometimes wondered, had we ended up living in such an enormous place? We had the problem of keeping it warm, especially during the winter months. The stone walls are over one metre thick and the flagstones have no damp-proof course. We soon found that if we left our wellington boots on the kitchen floor overnight there would be a wet patch underneath them in the morning! Fortunately, we could arrange our timer for the oil-fired central heating (which has five phases) to come on and off automatically in whatever room we were using and during our first two years we developed the stables into a two-up and one-down dream cottage.

Ten days after we moved in we held a three-day yoga retreat. Over twenty students, mostly from London, came to stay with us. It was September and to keep them warm we had every bit of heating on. The heating in the sitting room, which was under the flagstones, took five hours to come through. Though almost flat on top, the flagstones are like icebergs, with seven-eighths of their volume underneath, and the heating had to penetrate from this great depth. Old-fashioned radiators and the Aga cooker all went on. By the time the students left we had emptied the tank of oil, having used over 1000 litres in three days!

Yet one of the best things about living here is that it is really dark at night: showers of stars shine brightly while close by the owls too-wit too-woo. This is all very exciting when you have been living in London for thirty years.

One evening, as I was teaching my weekly yoga class in the village hall, who should appear but five Ishaya monks, our old friends from London; they had visited our last farmhouse and given talks to the yoga groups there. Dressed in white, their arrival began to cause some interest with the locals. After the class they came back to LHF and told us over supper that their plans had changed; they had moved out of London into a small terraced house in Crawley, a nearby village. Ten of them were living there and were rather squashed.

I remembered saying once to Ken and Angela how I would really love to have a big house somewhere in the country and to share it with the Ishayas. Well, it seemed obvious to us now what should happen. LHF became not only a yoga centre, but for four amazing years it was the Ishaya centre for the world. Quite unconsciously what I'd had in mind became manifest. The ten Ishaya monks moved in with us in November. Some of them joined in the weekly yoga classes in the village hall and two of them are now trained yoga teachers. It is part of their tradition that twice a day they practise yoga and also Ascend (meditate). It was such a pleasure to join them in this. Actually, it was a pleasure to see them at any time. The Ishayas express an attitude of love, which is catching. It's good to share and show your love, most of all when you don't feel like doing so.

Living with the Ishayas

A lot of changes occur when you are sharing with fellow Ishayas. For instance, there are plenty of beds but not always enough separate rooms, so you might be surprised to wake up and find you're sharing with women and men, all very respectful of each other's space. Meal times are very much a sharing experience, too, with giving of food rather than heaping up your own plate. Practice times are a great priority in the day and are very rarely missed and there is never a hesitation in giving or asking for help. I was not used to asking for help and found it difficult at times.

The 'attitude' teachings of the Ishayas are based on Love, Praise and Gratitude. The monks are invited into homes to teach for weekends and they sometimes give public talks. The four years that they spent with us at LHF were really special, while for them it was a record time to stay in one place for so long. The crime rate in the village went down, as happens wherever they live, and the villagers accepted them as 'normal' people. They couldn't resist their friendly ways, the Ishayas always helping where they could. Satta worked in the village pub and it wasn't unusual for the regulars to come back and share their problems with the Ishayas. It was open house.

The main changes for me were heart-lifting. It was the sort of feeling you have when you are on holiday or when you are a child; you wake up in the morning and feel it's good to be alive. You are free without burdens and in love with the world.

THE FIVE TIBETAN RITES OR EXERCISES

Here is a daily practice to keep you supple and strong. It also helps with balance. I like to practise first thing in the day as I find it brings the energy forward and quietens my mind. Begin by practising each rite two to seven times and then see if you can build up to twenty-one repetitions, whatever is comfortable for you.

Rite 1

Stand with your arms outstretched at shoulder height, palms facing down; with your feet a hip distance apart feel your full height, from the heels pressing down to the crown of the head ascending. Focus on a spot in front of you and start your clockwise rotations, turning your head to keep your gaze coming back to the spot. Spin round until you become a little dizzy; gradually increase the number of spins from two to twenty-one. Keep the breathing deep.

Rite 2

Lie flat on the floor and extend your arms along the sides of your body, palms down. As you exhale, lift your head while simultaneously lifting your straight legs until they are vertical. If you run out of breath stop the posture and continue on the next exhalation. Then slowly exhale, lowering your legs and then your head to the floor.

Rite 3

Kneel up from the floor with your toes turned under. Place your hands on the back of your thigh muscles and slide your hands down the back of your thighs as you draw your shoulder blades down. Lift your chin towards the sky. Roll your collar bones up, lifting your top chest. Hips forward, keep the lower back strong and straight. Keep breathing.

Rite 4

Sit down on the floor with your legs straight out in front of you with your feet about thirty centimetres apart. Place your palms on the floor alongside your sit bones. As you gently drop your head back, raise your torso by lifting your tailbone and top chest. Let your knees bend to a right angle; your arms are under your shoulders in table top position. Lifting your tail bone and top chest, slowly lower down to your original sitting position and repeat. Keep up the deep breathing.

Rite 5

Lie on your belly, hands either side of the chest. Press up into upward facing dog, legs straight. Bring your chest forwards, sinking in between your shoulder blades. Chin up (unless your neck hurts) and look up through the eyebrows. Next, bring hips back and up, with head down into downward facing dog. Repeat by moving back and forth between downward and upward facing dog. Don't hold the breath.

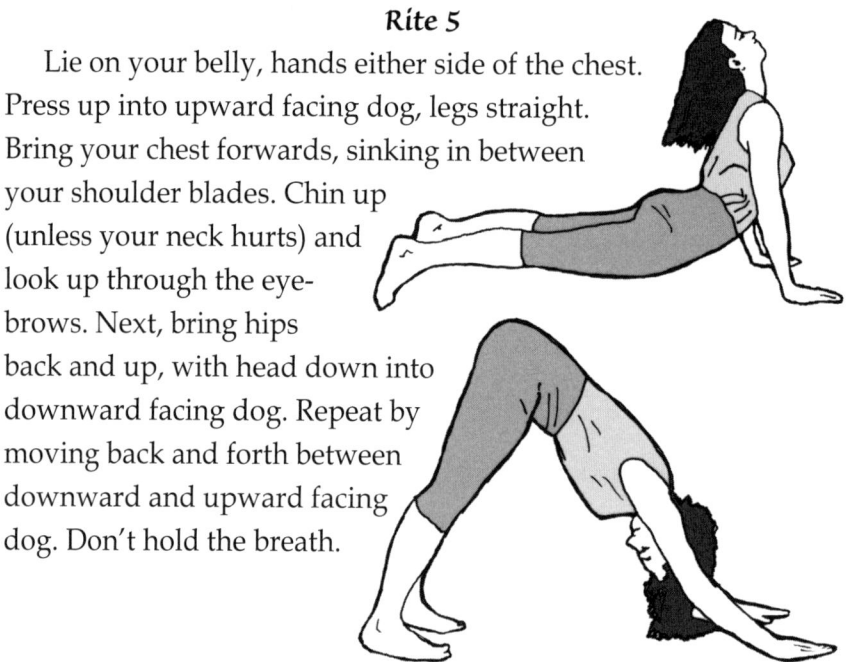

There is one more rite which needs to be taught first hand rather than given in written instruction as it is powerful and needs to be performed under guidance. Come to a yoga retreat and I will show you how it's done.

QUESTIONS AND ANSWERS WITH RUTH WHITE

From Yoga and Health magazine

Panic Attacks

Q. I have two small children and although I am quite well physically, every morning when I awake I feel an upsurge of panic about how I am going to cope and get through all the tasks of the day. My breathing changes and my mind starts to race. Sometimes I break out in perspiration. Can you help me please? I don't know how to stop it.

A. The best way to come back into the present is to give full attention to what you are doing. Lying on your mat, open your eyes and gaze around the room. Take your arms over the head and stretch well for longer than you would normally stretch. Deepen the breathing and listen to the sounds around you and right out to far distant sounds. Now get up and stretch back, legs in a dog posture (i.e. from a kneeling position, with hands forward on the floor giving support, lift the hips and let the head hang so that you have maximum stretch on the back of the legs and your back, hips maximum height. With practice, hold this for two minutes). Now remember, one thing at a time during the day. You can do it! Your children will respond well to your change in attitude. Your panic attacks will disappear if you bring your attention into the present. Yoga postures are a great way of synchronising mind and body into the present moment where panic attacks cannot exist. Spirit is always here and now.

Yoga for Mind, Body and Spirit

Q. Can you help me? I was persuaded to join a local yoga group when I really wanted to pursue a spiritual path, including meditation. I am told that yoga includes spiritual work, but I am finding it all rather physical. Could you help me to understand the body/spirit connection?

A. In understanding the spirit, the body is our greatest ally. Any movement in mind or spirit is reflected in the physical body. It may be so small that we don't see it, but it will be there. The body is a picture of the workings of the mind.

In yoga we are encouraged to listen to the body. Messages coming back are pleas for help, attention and, in most cases, a need for change. We tend to ignore these messages and plough on, taking an aspirin for a headache or a cup of coffee when the body is requiring rest.

These pleas we receive from the physical body are tremendously informative, but we need practice in listening and strength of will to carry out what we know would be the best way to bring body and mind into harmony.

Watch the children when they are tired. They go to sleep wherever they are. When they have had enough to eat, they push their plates away and, very importantly, when they wake up they want to get up straight away, not lie in a dream world losing energy. Compare that to the Sunday morning 'sleep in' when we surface and wake up at our natural time but, ignoring this, we snuggle down in a half-sleep and by the time we do get up, maybe hours later, feel quite shattered.

There is a natural measure for all of this if we can tune into this informative body we happen to inhabit. All energy and measure are there.

This unlimited information surrounds us all. It is eternal and available at any time, but we need to be able to tune in. All we have to do is to listen. To really listen we need to allow the busy mind to fall quiet so that we can come into the present and allow this information in.

As we begin to spend more time in the present and less time in dreaming about past or future events, we get better at listening. The senses refine and we begin to feel and hear the warning signs before the physical symptoms occur. For example, I feel a slight tightening and drying of the skin just before a cold appears, a tightening of the scalp if I am dehydrated or a gut reaction to unhelpful foods *before* I have eaten them.

Yoga is an excellent way of cutting through our prejudices and opinions. Yoga works on all levels – mind, body and spirit. It must be so, otherwise body tension can only be temporarily and partially removed. This is why the body/spirit connection cannot be separated.

Taming the Scattered Mind

Q. I have always had a lot of energy but I tend to be a bit scatty. I find it difficult to concentrate on one thing for long. I hold down an easy job and have lots of friends but if I am in for the evening alone, I cannot stop nibbling. I am not too large at the moment but I feel I may end up enormous if I continue to do this. I am a bit ashamed of this desire to eat and only succumb when I am on my own. Any suggestions please?

A. A desire may arise in the mind for food. We think it is physical and yet, when we start to eat, it is not satisfying, so we find more to eat, hoping the desire will diminish. It does not, because the desire has not been truly satisfied. It takes a lot of willpower sometimes to turn away from pleasure and quieten the agitation in the mind, the 'want it/get it' syndrome. Choose something that you feel at harmony doing, such as listening to your favourite music, or taking a walk, and give your full attention to it. Sit quietly in a comfortable position with the back straight, close your eyes and relax. Place your hands, palms facing upwards. Keep the face soft, release the neck, the top of the shoulders and upper arms. Please do not force the breath or strain and move back into normal breathing when you feel the body has had enough. The maximum time for this practice to begin with should be ten minutes.

Q. I am quite fit, but, for no particular reason at all, I just feel down and depressed. I am a nurse and work night shifts. Can you help?

A. You spend your time caring for others and maybe stooping over beds. The postures that would help to lift depression are the postures that lift and open the emotional centre – the heart. When standing, sitting or lying, straighten the back and lift the chest, rolling the collar bones towards the ears. Now tighten the pelvic floor so that the inner abdominal area moves up towards the chest. Straighten the head and starting with an exhalation, deepen your breathing. You can practise this when walking.

A yoga class would greatly help as the practice of yoga has the effect of unblocking the streams of *prana* (life energy) which travel around the body. Depression is usually caused by low energy and, as you know, the practice of *pranayama* or deep breathing increases oxygen levels which has an effect on the whole body, including the mind. You will find that, as the energy in the body is lifted and balanced, the depression will also lift. Be disciplined about your sleeping patterns. You do not necessarily have to sleep for very long but you do need deep, uninterrupted sleep. A good time to practise yoga may be before going to sleep (using the seated postures) and using the stretching and standing postures when you wake up. You have a great opportunity in your profession to open your heart to others which is the way to lighten your own.

Q. I have been teaching a new group of students and one of the participants suffers from migraine. How would you handle this type of problem?

A. With regard to this problem, migraine is caused by stuck energy. Taking the head down will increase the flow of blood to the head. As Iyengar would say, any inverted posture is a tonic for the head. Sports such as swimming or table tennis can help move the energy.

QUESTIONS FOR THE READER

Perhaps reading this book has changed your mind about the way you experience the world. See if your attitude has changed by pondering and responding to these questions:

1) What do I want more than anything else?
2) How is my relationship with others?
3) What am I compromising on in my life?
4) Do I want to be right or happy?
5) What do I experience when my mind quietens and my heart opens?

RECOMMENDED BOOKS

Light on Yoga. Author: B.K.S. Iyengar (Harper Thorsons)

Chit Happens: A Guide to Discovering Divinity. Author: Narain Ishaya (Balboa Press)

Good Company. An Anthology of sayings, stories and answers to questions by His Holiness Sri Shantanand Saraswati, Shankaracharya of Jyotir Math (Element Books)

I Am That. Sri Nisargadatta Maharaj (Chetana Ltd.)

The Power of Now. Author: Eckhart Tolle (Hodder & Stoughton)

A Course in Miracles. Author: Dr Helen Schucman (Foundation for Inner Peace)

The Disappearance of the Universe. Author: Gary R. Renard (Hay House)

Autobiography of a Yogi. Author: Paramahansa Yogananda (Self-Realization Fellowship)

CDs and DVDs by Ruth White:
Complete Yoga Audio (CD)
Yoga Positions (DVD)
Yoga Back Stretches (DVD)
Yoga for the More Adept (DVD)
Yoga for Pregnancy (DVD)

For information about yoga retreats, teacher training courses and regular yoga classes run by Ruth White please visit her website: www.yogawithruthwhite.com

'The still mind finds peace in everything.'

PERSONAL NOTES

ONE OF MANY GOOD REVIEWS

PRESENCE · The Truth of Yoga is very different from most books on the subject. Ruth White's point of view challenges us to examine the truth about yoga, offering tremendous insight into its meaning and inviting us to explore horizons beyond familiar territory.

This well written book is a pleasure to read. While including every aspect of yoga it also clarifies some misconceptions about its practice. The title itself delves into the nature of yoga and how the universe aligns itself to bring harmony into the lives of those who practise it.

It is one of the few books that takes the reader into the realm of the spiritual – the *Samadhi*, yoga's ultimate aim. It is like embarking on a personal journey, discovering the depth of the inner self. This brings about a balance between body, mind and spirit.

Ruth explains how yoga brings suppleness to the body and a sense of well-being. Written through many years of teaching yoga, she offers tips to help both beginners and expert yogis find a way of life that is adapted to modern living.

This book is a testimony to Ruth's experience as a yoga teacher. We all know that yoga equals or surpasses other types of exercise in terms of improving balance, lifting moods, reducing fatigue and generally raising the quality of one's life, etc., yet *PRESENCE* touches on truths that affect people in a way that is sublime.

It will appeal to beginners, professionals and non-yogis alike, offering a window that opens to the higher aspirations of yoga. We only need to clear the cobwebs of our hearts and minds in order to see more clearly and be receptive to the truths that yoga has to offer.

Sister Evelyn – *Former Superior General of the Franciscan Order of St Mary of the Angels.*